Shane Warne

MY OWN STORY

Shane Warne

MY OWN STORY

As told to MARK RAY

SWAN
PUBLISHING

Acknowledgments

Shane Warne gratefully acknowledges the following people and organisations for their generous assistance in providing the photographs for My Own Story.

Trent Parke, Mark Ray, Viv Jenkins, Steve Cuff, David Evans and Ray Titus. Also John Fairfax, News Ltd., Australian Picture Library/All Sport, SPORT. The Library, Australian Cricket Board, Inside Edge/PBL Marketing.

Some photos in this book are from Shane Warne's personal collection; they have been kindly offered to Shane by cricket photographers from around the world and include Danie Coetzer in Johannesburg.

Designer: Stan Lamond, Lamond Art & Design

Copy-editor: Dawn Koester

First published in 1997 by
Swan Publishing Pty Ltd
Suite 14C, 81 Waratah Ave. Dalkeith, W.A. 6009
Copyright © 1997
Swan Publishing Ltd
This book is copyright, apart from any fair dealing for the purposes of private study, research, criticism or reviews, as permitted under the Copyright Act, no part may be reproduced by any process without written permission. Inquiries should be addressed to the publishers.
National Library of Australia
Cataloguing-in-Publication data
Ray, Mark,.
Shane Warne : my own story.
ISBN 0 9586760 1 1.
1. Warne, Shane. 2. Cricket players - Australia - Biography. I. Title.
796.358092

Printed in Australia by McPherson's Printing Group

Page 1: David Callow/Sport. The Library
Page 2: Niels Schipper/Australian Picture Library
Pages 4/5: Mark Ray

Contents

One of the most common questions I get asked during the cricket season, apart from "How's Mark going?", is "What's Warnie really like?"

Each time I give them the answer, they usually reply, "Is that right? I'm glad to hear that."

Warnie is a once-in-a-generation player, perhaps even a once-in-a-lifetime player, who as such is always going to be judged on his every move. He has such a high profile that cricket enjoys many benefits that emanate from his presence, but with this package also comes the inevitable knockers who like to take a champion down at every opportunity just to create a bit of publicity or to sell a few more papers.

All I know from having played with Shane is that Australian cricket is fortunate to have him, for he can win Test matches single handedly, he will guarantee that crowds flock to the cricket to see him and he ignites the passion amongst the youngsters who want to emulate his deeds and every move. Surprisingly, this all comes from a man who basically lives on toasted cheese sand-

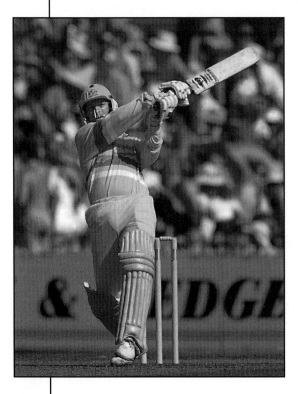

wiches, spaghetti bolognaise, french fries and bread rolls smothered with butter, whose taste in music that includes favourites such as Leo Sayer, Boney M and ABBA, whilst admiring such heroes as The Undertaker and Hulk Hogan. You see, Warnie is just like the average Aussie guy. He's approachable, looks after his mates, is humble, unselfish, generous, enjoys the success of others, is team oriented and loyal, and that more so than his deeds makes him a special person!

STEVE WAUGH

Don Bradman, in his book *My Cricketing Life*, describes one of his great moments in Adelaide in 1937 when 'Chuck' Fleetwood-Smith bowled Wally Hammond, something Bradman had prefaced with the words, "Chuck, if ever Australia needed a super effort from you, it's now."

It was described as a ball that *swerved away from the right-hander and then curled inside his perfect defensive stroke, and hit the stumps.* It also squared a series at 2–2 after Australia had lost the first two Tests in Brisbane and Sydney. That ball to level a Test series became legendary in Australian cricket, as did the one with which Shane Warne influenced the 1993 series when, at Old Trafford, he dismissed Mike Gatting with his first ball in a Test in England.

That dismissal was with a ball that *started on middle and off and then, after swerving to pitch just outside leg-stump, whipped back and took the off-bail. Many have said it spun two feet and was unplayable.* In fact it only spun about fourteen inches and was almost unplayable. It will forever be a part of Australia's cricket lore because, through television, more than a billion people have seen it.

It is hardly more than a couple of blinks since Warne began a Test career with his first 90 overs costing 335 runs for a solitary wicket; in the following seven years he has changed the face of the game, mainly because he is an exponent of what seemed to be a fascinating but dying art. He has had a few hiccups along the way, has delighted and enthralled spectators and television viewers and has allowed full rein to radio commentators and newspaper reporters.

His book, covering seven years where he has been the best young leg-spinner I have ever seen, deserves to go well. Now, after two tours of England and a severe finger injury that at one stage seemed certain to terminate his career, he faces further challenges. How he meets them will greatly influence Australia's dominance, or otherwise, in international cricket.

RICHIE BENAUD

Shane Warne was selected, out of the blue, to play for Australia against India at the SCG in 1991.

It was no fairytale beginning. Shanes figures of 1/150 were less than flattering, prompting Kerry O'Keeffe, a great student and critic of the game to write in his notebook, after seeing this young upstart for the first time, "Overweight, slightly roundarm, no variation, can't bowl." Kerry takes great delight in recounting those first impressions.

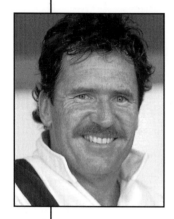

On the other hand, I was very impressed, not so much by the results, but by something about Shane himself — his attitude, confidence and willingness to listen that struck a chord with me.

Warnie had the next winter off and took it upon himself to get fit and seek advice, especially from Terry Jenner. Shane Warne turned up at our pre-season camp trim, hair cropped short with a hint of bleach (he still maintains it's natural) plus the now famous earring. He looked a million dollars.

Still, success didn't come immediately. The Sri Lankans had taken to Shane's new-look bowling. It wasn't until the second innings of the First Test in Colombo that we saw the first signs of something special. With the Sri Lankans needing 30 odd to win, still four wickets in hand, I threw the ball to Warnie. It was a huge gamble. He looked a little shocked to get the ball but said he was ready for the job. It's history now that Warnie, along with Greg Matthews, took those last wickets. We won a Test we shouldn't have and the Warne legend was born.

For me personally, and for Australian cricket, Shane was like a breath of fresh air. He added a spark to everyone with his attitude and his bowling. My own captaincy flourished and as I look on now, I realise how lucky we are to have him.

ALLAN BORDER

The first time I heard about Shane Warne it was from former Australian wicketkeeper Brian Taber. As manager of the Australian youth team that toured the Caribbean in 1990, Brian summed up the young leg-spinner this way: "Most of the other guys [in the team] didn't want to know about drinking with the opposition after facing a few bouncers, but Shane would always grab a bottle of beer and march into their room and chat away happily after a day's play. He's also not a bad leg-spinner."

Apart from developing into one of cricket's finest leg-spinners, not much about Shane has changed since those days in the Caribbean. He still has a great love for the game and its traditions and he enjoys talking about cricket as well as playing it to the best of his ability. Warne, along with Sachin Tendulkar has handled fame and adulation in an extremely mature fashion. The way Shane treats young fans is indicative of a man who still vividly recalls his own cricketing roots.

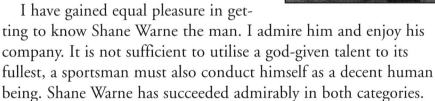

I have enjoyed watching the development of Shane Warne into a great Test match bowler, possessed of a keen cricket brain and a strong competitive spirit. My only disappointment would be if he shied away from taking on the Australian captaincy while he is still at his peak as a player. I think he would make a fine leader in the most difficult category of all, a bowling captain.

I have gained equal pleasure in getting to know Shane Warne the man. I admire him and enjoy his company. It is not sufficient to utilise a god-given talent to its fullest, a sportsman must also conduct himself as a decent human being. Shane Warne has succeeded admirably in both categories.

IAN CHAPPELL

The only other time I saw that look on Mike Gatting's face was when he discovered someone had pinched his lunch.

More than enough words to fill this book have been written about that day in 1993 at Old Trafford, Manchester, when Shane Warne announced his arrival to the English cricket public by unleashing the ball from hell to the unsuspecting Gatt.

All I'd like to say is that I'm glad he didn't bowl it at me.

I am full of admiration for Shane's bowling, and in my opinion he has been without doubt the brightest spin-bowling talent to emerge in the past quarter of a century, perhaps even of all time. Not only that, I cannot believe how easily he has taken in his stride the business of being one of the most high-profile celebrities in world sport.

I've always found that, with Shane, what you see is what you get, a bloke totally unfazed and unaffected not only by what he has achieved but also by what he has become.

I first really got to know him when we worked together on a commercial for Nike and how right they were to pair quite probably the two finest examples of lean athleticism in world sport.

It was during this experience that I learned the reasons behind Warne's extraordinary physique. For I'm dead certain that if you offered to take him for a meal of his choice in any of the finest restaurants in the world, the decision would ultimately hinge on one thing only; which of them served the best pizza.

Now his everything-but-pasta-free diet is not exactly what the nutritionalists would recommend for our top sportsmen, but, like someone else I know, Shane has never been one to do thing by the book and that goes a long way to explaining his immense worldwide appeal.

A top man, is Warnie and, above all, the same as he ever was. Australian cricket, come to that, world cricket should be thankful we have him.

IAN BOTHAM

How great it is, to witness the hustling, bustling blond ball of body language, systematically gluing batsmen's feet to the crease, minimising their willingness to innovate against such big spinning leggies. The confidence and variety that this scenario gives to our team have been responsible for a high proportion of our victories in such a successful period. Last-day survival plans become most impossible by even the world's best when Warnie spins his magic.

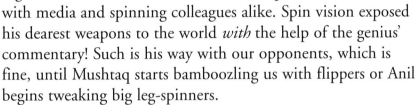

Warnie's on-field genius aside, he has the team's fortunes at heart, which is so inspirational it wins the most experienced of us. Such a craftsman is entitled to a high level of secrecy regarding his trade, but I admire Shane's total openness with media and spinning colleagues alike. Spin vision exposed his dearest weapons to the world *with* the help of the genius' commentary! Such is his way with our opponents, which is fine, until Mushtaq starts bamboozling us with flippers or Anil begins tweaking big leg-spinners.

Shane Warne has a great ability to cope with the spotlight, remember his roots and old mates, as well as motivate others around him. Warnie is never far from the action, which will make this story not only an interesting one, but I believe a valuable one for many.

Bowled Warnie.

IAN HEALY

I am delighted that Shane Warne has asked me to write a fore-word to his first book.

The world wants and needs its sporting superstars. They challenge their teammates and competitors. They please their sponsors and, indirectly, sell products. They provide great enter-tainment, not only to their supporters but to the sporting public generally. They inspire all of us and particularly the young.

There is no doubt that Shane is a cricketing superstar. Al-though his career has so long to go, he has achieved so much already. He has revitalised the art of leg-spinning and already his name is up there with the spinning greats, including Clarrie Grimmett, Bill O'Reilly and Richie Benaud. I believe that when Shane's career is finally at an end, his name and place among the top rank of cricket's hierarchy will be secured.

However, others seem better qualified than me to write of Shane the cricketer. I would like to make some comments about Shane the man. In the Australian vernacular, Shane is a 'good bloke' and I am proud to call him a friend. On the field he is

fiercely competitive, as I am sure his opponents will attest. However, off it, he is a great compan-ion, not only to his own teammates but to the opposing players too. Like many Australians, he enjoys a laugh, a drink and a bet.

Shane has earned the respect of his teammates and opposition players. He is clearly a student of cricket. He has been astoundingly successful and he is extraordinarily popular with the Australian public and cricket lovers around the world; yet he remains the same unassuming young man he was when he first burst onto the cricket scene.

This book, which essentially is of Shane's life story to date, is both interesting and entertaining. I commend it to cricket lovers and all Australians.

James D Packer

Every now and then a sportsman captures the sporting world's imagination with his skill and expertise as well as his off-field demeanour, behaviour and community standing.

Shane Warne is that sort of charismatic and endearing character, a man who has taken a most difficult skill, wrist spin bowling and catapulted its bench mark to a new level. The way top level players from sports other than cricket speak reverently about Shane is an indication of the high regard he is held in on the world sporting stage.

I have known Shane socially and professionally for a number of years and he's always portrayed a modest and humble approach to his spiralling cricket career and always finds time to sign autographs for his fans, especially young children.

Shane is one of a select few players who will be remembered for one delivery as much as for his outstanding cricket career — the Gatting ball that people around the world still talk about.

There has already been a couple of unauthorised biographies on Shane's career and no doubt others will follow. His concern about stories being embellished has prompted this book.

I am proud to call Shane a true friend and only hope he retains the enthusiasm and desire to continue and succeed at the highest level, because he has been a revelation to Test cricket at a time when perhaps the one-day game was beginning to appeal to the next generation of cricketers.

With the right amount of good fortune Shane can become the first and maybe the only bowler to take 500 Test wickets. No one who has run from the car park at the cricket when they've heard the gatekeeper say, "Warnie's on!" would begrudge the greatest leg-spinner in the history of the game that hitherto unthinkable milestone.

LLOYD WILLIAMS

Under the Knife

Often the only times I have a chance to relax on my own and do some thinking is late at night at home in Melbourne. During those increasingly rare months away from cricket and touring life, I tend to sit up late and just enjoy the peace and quiet and the free time. The winter of 1996, after the Australian team came back from the World Cup in India and Pakistan, should've been one of those times. Plenty of golf, time to catch up with friends around Melbourne and the trip to America that combined some work for Channel 9 at the US Masters with a holiday with my wife Simone.

Although I did manage to do all of that, it was not the pleasant period I'd wanted and needed. I had things on my mind — a sore spinning finger and a sore shoulder. And after I'd made one of the toughest decisions of my life — to have surgery on the finger — those late nights were not exactly relaxing. There were plenty of occasions when I sat up late, knowing I wouldn't be able to go to sleep for another few hours, and when all I could think of was whether I'd ever play for Australia again. It was a long winter.

My finger, the third on the hand and the one which straightens with a snap to give the ball a decent flick, first began to show signs of trouble during the tour to the West Indies in 1995. That tour came immediately after the Ashes series in Australia in 1994–5 and I thought the finger was merely showing signs of early wear and tear. It felt fine during the early stages of the series against Pakistan the following home summer, but during the second series, against Sri Lanka, it started to feel sore at the end of a day in the field. By the Third Test in Adelaide it was very sore. During the season I'd been forced to have cortisone injections straight into the knuckle. I'm no hero when it comes to needles and it hurt like hell when the doctor wriggled the needle around inside the knuckle. The injections were meant to last about six weeks but by Adelaide they were working for only two weeks.

The series against Sri Lanka was followed by the World Cup. In one-day cricket you only bowl 10 overs a game instead of maybe 50 in a five-day Test. But in a one-day series you are still playing often and practising in between matches. The workload is intense although I have tended to reduce the amount of serious bowling I do at net sessions over the years. Often I'll rest my finger and shoulder by just bowling some gentle medium-pacers. As long as my form is good there is no desperate need to bowl proper leggies at practice.

My finger was fine during the early matches of the World Cup but by quarter-final time it had deteriorated badly. At practice in Madras the day before the quarter-final against New Zealand my finger blew up. The veins started popping out through the knuckle. I called over our physiotherapist, Errol Alcott who was amazed by what he saw. He massaged my forearm and hand and said they were very tight. Right at the crucial stage of the World Cup my finger looked like collapsing altogether.

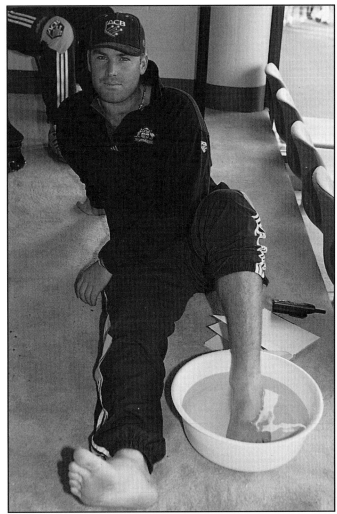

Wet nursing a cracked big toe, courtesy of Waqar Younis's famous yorker during the Second Test against Pakistan in Hobart, 1995. More troubled times, physically, were just around the corner.

SHAUN BOTTERILL/ALL SPORT

With Errol's help I got through the tournament, but when I returned home I decided I had to do something about the finger. I did not want to continue with the cortisone injections. They have side-effects and they were losing their effect anyway. Most former leg-spinners I spoke to said that an operation was the last resort, that the finger would never be the same after surgery, that it might even end up too stiff to bowl much at all.

During the trip to the US I visited a shoulder and finger specialist in Los Angeles. The message was simple enough: the shoulder specialist recommended surgery; the finger specialist thought all I needed was a few months rest. Sorry gents, but I knew that would not happen. The finger had been playing up for 12 months and nothing I'd tried had eased the pain for more than a few weeks at a time. The months after the World Cup were going to be the only decent stretch of free time I would have for more than a year. Either I'd take that chance to have the operation and use the spare time to work hard on the recuperation, or I'd have to keep going the way I had been with the finger likely to deteriorate quickly until my career was finished a few years earlier than expected.

If I had the operation there was always the chance I might not bowl again or that I would never be able to bowl the same as I had been. But in the series against Sri Lanka and then in the World Cup I'd had to be careful about bowling my big leg-break too often. That is my stock ball and my best ball, the one around which everything else in my bowling revolves. Lose that and for me the fun goes out of bowling. There is nothing better for a spinner than to see a ball spin sharply from one side of the pitch to the other, right past a stunned batsman. I did not want to change into another sort of leg-spinner. Either I kept bowling like Shane Warne or I'd have to go off and do something else.

In the end I decided to have surgery on the finger but not on the shoulder. With the shoulder I did all the physio work as if I'd had the operation but the knife only touched the finger. The morning of the operation the Victorian Cricket Association announced that I was to be the new Victorian captain in place of Dean Jones, who had fallen out of favour. That afternoon, 21 May, I checked into a private sports clinic in Melbourne wondering what sort of shape I'd be in after the operation. Would I be able to fulfil a dream and actually captain Victoria? Would I ever play for Australia again? My rise to the Test team had happened so quickly that I didn't know much else. To have it taken away just when my career was about to take another step forward with the state captaincy would have been the worst blow of my life. But there was no choice. I had to have the operation and

Coming to grips with reality — would I be the same bowler after my finger operation?

JACK ATLEY/THE AGE

then work as hard as possible to get the finger back to normal during the rest of the winter. The West Indies were coming to Australia to try to re-gain the Frank Worrell Trophy we took from them in the Caribbean the year before. I wanted to be part of Australia's campaign to beat them and to prove we were the best Test team in the world.

I could not have come through the operation and the recuperation without the help of the surgeon, Greg Hoy, and the physio, Debbie Benger, both of whom copped a lot of criticism and more advice than a politician during an election campaign. Despite the pressure they were under, they remained positive and kept encouraging me. At times it seemed that everyone I spoke to — from friends and teammates in Melbourne, to people in the street to journalists and radio and television reporters — wanted to know one thing: "How is your finger?" I appreciated their concern but I soon got sick of answering the question. There was not much I could say anyway. I was doing all the rehabilitation work I'd been given. I was seeing Debbie three or four times a week and doing all the exercises she gave me. I often had to wear a brace on my finger which kept the middle knuckle fully bent. To me, the one thing I needed, if and when the finger was good enough for me to bowl pre-season, was to rebuild my confidence in it. I said that to most people but I wasn't sure they believed me, or if I believed myself.

Although things seemed to go well during the winter rehabilitation, I was not exactly back to form in my first game, a match for my club St Kilda at the start of the 1996–7 Melbourne season. I struggled to bowl and got hammered. The finger was still stiff and I was unsure about how to let the ball come out of the hand. Although I did not say so publicly, I knew I had no chance of making the team to tour Sri Lanka for some one-day games in August. There was also a tour to India in October for one Test in Delhi and some one-dayers. I was hoping to make that tour but I was not too confident. The most important thing was to be fit and in good enough form to be chosen for the First Test against the West Indies in Brisbane in November.

In my first game for Victoria, as captain this time, I bowled an average spell in a one-day game in Adelaide against South Australia. Jamie Siddons charged me early on and missed, but other than that I did not exactly bowl well. I wasn't an embarrassment but I was a long way from my best. The future still seemed uncertain.

In the end I stayed behind in Melbourne as the Australian team left for India. It was the first Test match I'd missed since I was not selected for the First against the West Indies at the start of the 1992–3 season. It especially hurt because I was very keen to go to India, as my Test debut was against them in Sydney in 1991–2. I didn't have a great game and I'd not played against them since that series. As well, the pitches in India suit spin and Indian cricket has produced some of the game's greatest spinners. Any spin bowler would love to play a Test match in India.

While the Australians were in India I took five wickets in a one-day game against Tasmania in Melbourne which boosted my confidence and then, a few weeks later, bowled 45 overs in a Sheffield Shield game against New South Wales in Sydney. I was not turning or dipping the ball like I used to, but my accuracy was improving and I was at least able to bowl long spells. The finger was improving every week and I was on course for the First Test.

After lots of consultations with Errol Alcott, new Australian team coach Geoff Marsh and chairman of selectors Trevor Hohns, I was chosen for the First Test and went on to take 22 wickets in the series. Although I was a little tentative in that first match, I felt I bowled my best for that summer in the next Test, in Sydney a week later. A net session with Terry Jenner before that game helped my confidence and got me propelling the ball properly out of the hand rather than just putting it there as I had done in Brisbane.

Although I did not take a five-wicket haul in the series I felt I bowled well. Glenn McGrath won the Player of the Series award and received great praise for his bowling — which he fully deserved — but he took only four more wickets than I did, yet people were saying I'd had a disappointing series. I wasn't disappointed. I was delighted. Three of the Test matches were over in three days and two of those were played on pitches that suited fast bowlers much more than spinners. I'd have taken more wickets in Adelaide if Michael Bevan had not wrapped up the tail so quickly. Some of those wickets would have been mine, but I'm happy for Bev to be taking wickets at the other end. It had been a while since I'd had Tim May bowling spin at the other end to me and I always prefer bowling in tandem with another spinner. If Bev continues to bowl well, and I think he will, he will ease the pressure on me and hopefully that will mean I'll be able to play with fewer injuries and for longer than I would have as the one spinner. As well as good form, I was pleased with the way my finger had come through with no further deterioration. It was sore after a day's bowling but I knew that would be the case and gradually I got used to it. At least I was back contributing to the Australian cricket team.

After every day's bowling I have a massage session with Errol which releases the tension in my shoulder, forearm and hand. It is quite a while before I can relax and have a beer, but the massage certainly helps all those muscles that have been twisting and turning maybe 200 times that day.

Although I bowled well in the Sydney and Adelaide Tests against the West Indies and so played my part in a great series win, it was in the First Test against South Africa in Johannesburg that I really bowled near my best. Although the pitch was very slow, I spun the ball a long way in the second innings and at a brisk enough pace to prove that I was putting a lot of work on the ball at the time of release from my hand. That was the closest I'd come to my old bowling style since the operation. It was a crucial Test match, the first of an important series, and we badly wanted to beat South Africa

TRENT PARKE/NEWS LTD

SHAUN BOTTERILL/ALL SPORT

LEFT: Turning the corner. A net session with my mentor and friend Terry Jenner, the former Australian leg-spinner, made all the difference after my bowling had lacked its old zip in the early comeback games following my finger operation. It was at the SCG, before the Second Test against the West Indies in 1996.

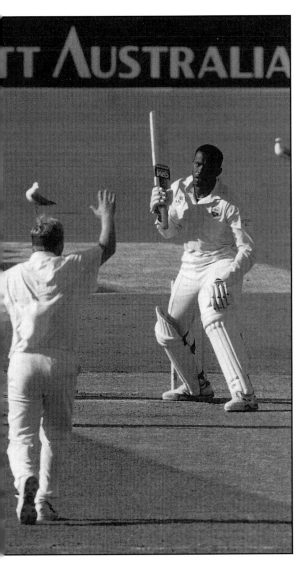

LEFT: **Body language. By the Fourth Test of the 1996-7 series against the West Indies, in Adelaide, I was almost back to my best. The victim is Ian Bishop, one of six for the match.**

first up to damage their confidence. It was my 50th Test and it was played on the same ground where three years earlier I'd misbehaved and been punished by the International Cricket Council referee and then by the Australian Cricket Board. I had ground to make up and things to prove in that game and I think I managed to do both. I worried my old bunny from the 1994–5 series in Australia, Darryl Cullinan, in the first innings and got him for a duck in the second and I even bowled one batsman, Jacques Kallis, behind his legs just as I used to do in the days before my operation.

It seemed that my finger was going to be alright and that my form would be back to normal for the Ashes series in England a few months after the South Africa series. The finger problem, the operation on it and the months afterwards had been the toughest of my cricket life. With the help and the support of a lot of people — my wife, my family, my doctor and physio, the team physio, Terry Jenner and my teammates — I made it through to the other end of what at times had seemed like a dark and very long tunnel. It was not easy, but international cricket is my life at the moment and I had to do everything I could to come through this and continue my career. Simone was fantastic support throughout. There were plenty of days when I'd be grumpy about the slow recovery of my finger. In between all these low days, there were others when I'd come home and hug her in delight because I'd managed to bowl a leg-break at practice that afternoon. Simone always understood what I was going through and was able to put up with my mood swings.

Early Days

Towards the end of August 1990 I was a long way from the southern suburbs of my home town, Melbourne. At one stage I found myself on a rickety old wooden bus in Guyana with the Australian youth team. We were in the Caribbean for a month-long tour that included three Youth Tests. I'd been to England in 1989 but this was my first official cricket tour and, for a bloke still only 20 years old, it was an eye-opening experience.

That bus managed to take the Australian and West Indies youth teams and all our gear miles and miles until we reached a beautiful river, wide and impressive. People were washing in it and probably doing anything else they wanted or needed to do. It looked terrific until we realised we had to climb on board a couple of canoes and start across to the other shore. The canoes were made for 15 people but I reckon we had up to 30 on ours as well as a couple of dozen coffins full of cricket gear. It was a scary ride but we made it alright before getting into a wooden bus for another long ride to a ground somewhere in what seemed like a jungle. After all, Guyana is on mainland South America.

When we got to the ground the whole area was saturated and there were people everywhere soaking up the water with sponges and anything else that worked. In the end we managed to give them a game of cricket although it was not like any I'd played back in Australia. That trip and the one to Zimbabwe the following year were my introduction to international cricket, if you like. It was not at the top level, but all of us in the Youth Team knew in the back of our minds that the selectors were watching our progress. Sixteen months later I would play my first Test match, against India at the Sydney Cricket Ground. It was a sudden rise, especially for a chubby young kid who had only ever wanted to play Australian Rules football.

My heroes in Aussie Rules were Hawthorn's great centre half-forward Dermott Brereton and St Kilda's Trevor Barker. Trevor played for my club, St Kilda and was a brilliant, spectacular mark. He was very popular around the club and in later years we became good friends. His early death from cancer was an awful tragedy and I'm sure it made all of those people who

LEFT & BELOW:
I had other sporting
instincts when I was young.

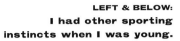

My career with St Kilda Under-19s and Reserves was shortlived.

had the honour to know him realise how brief lives and careers can be. Trevor gave a lot of pleasure to a lot of people and will always remain one of my heroes.

Brereton played footy with flair and pride. He was a bit of a larrikin and his sense of fun appealed to me as much as his courage and skill. But I did not quite have what it took to make it to the AFL. I made St Kilda's Under-19s and played one game in the reserves, but I lacked pace and was dropped from the list at the start of the 1989 season. It was a major blow, a real kick in the guts, the end of a boyhood dream. All I'd wanted as a kid was to play senior footy and I'd nearly made it, but now I had to look elsewhere. I loved team sports and the friendships you made through them and I'd always played cricket, so it looked like I'd have to have a go at that instead of footy.

Not long after that setback I won a scholarship to the Australian Institute of Sport Cricket Academy in Adelaide. Maybe things were starting to work for me in cricket. Australia had not had many top class leg-spinners for quite a few years. Some people in the game even thought leggies were just about an extinct species, but there were also people who knew that leg-spinners had done a lot for Australian cricket over the years and that Australia had led the world in producing wrist spinners. People like Victoria's Test selector Jim Higgs, himself a former Australian leg-spinner, were always on the lookout for a promising young leggie and I suppose I received that scholarship because of the Australian game's desire to find another leggie. And even though the Academy and I had our differences, it was an important experience and led to those two overseas Youth tours.

The Australian Youth Team that went to the Caribbean in 1990 contained names that are still around: Jamie Cox (captain), Craig White and Jason Gallian (who went on to play Test cricket for England), Michael Bevan, Damien Martyn, Brendon Julian, Darren Berry, Damien Fleming, Shane George, Chris Mack, David Castle, Stuart Oliver, Jason Young and myself. All of those guys have played first-class cricket and seven out of the 14 made it to Test cricket.

During the West Indies v Victoria game in Wangaratta before Christmas 1996, a photograph appeared in *The Age* showing Damien Fleming roaring with laughter at something Sherwin Campbell had said. It was no surprise that the photo showed them as old mates. They got to know each other on that Youth tour to the West Indies in 1990. Sherwin was captain of the West Indies side and I spent a fair bit of time with him off the field. Although there was some aggro in a few of the games, I got on well with

DAVID EVANS/PORT DOUGLAS

My love of Australian Rules is as fierce as ever. I found some friends
at the **Super-8s** in Cairns before the 1996-7 season. I took the mark!

their players and enjoyed spending time with them and letting them show me the sights and the nightlife.

At the end of the tour one of the West Indian officials presented me with a Friendship Award. It was a surprise to me then and probably is now to people who have seen me show some aggression to an opposing batsman. But that award did mean a lot to me and still does. The person you see on the field who often gets pretty fired up in the heat of competition is different to the one off the field. I might be fierce out on the ground, but off it I try to get to know opposition players and I've managed to make many friends around the cricket world. After all, we're playing a game we love. We all have that in common and most cricketers are good people. As a kid I'd always enjoyed the company of teammates and at St Kilda Cricket Club I learned a lot about being in a team, being part of a club and about getting on with the opposition after a game. Also I saw how the older guys at St Kilda mixed with the guys from the other clubs. They'd all get together after a game and have a beer and a chat. I enjoyed that scene. When I started touring and playing senior cricket it just seemed the natural thing to do.

I think the friendships you make out of cricket are important because in 10 years time, when you're having a few people over for a barbecue, most of them will be guys you've played cricket with. They are generally your best mates. They are there for you when you need them because they have been through the same experiences and understand what pressures are put on you. When you play as much cricket as we do, those experiences and friendships intensify and, sadly in a way, you don't have that much time to make friends outside cricket. These days I really only have a few mates from outside the game. As a professional cricketer I have so little spare time that in the past few years I've lost track of a few close school friends. I suppose it often happens as people start careers, marry and move on in life, but it's also disappointing if you value friendships as much as I do.

There is one other reason to go in and have a beer with the opposition after a day's play: you just might hear something or gain a piece of information that could give you an edge on the opposition next time you meet them on the field.

After the tour to the West Indies and my time at the Academy I made my debut for Victoria during 1990–1. At the end of that summer I decided to go back to England to play another season of league cricket. I'd been dropped from the Victorian side at the end of the 1990–1 season, when Victoria won the Shield. It was disappointing not to be part of that victory on the Melbourne Cricket Ground against traditional rivals New South Wales, but I still paid my couple of dollars and went with my brother Jason to watch the games. But I'd had a taste of playing at that level and I wanted more. A day at the cricket with a few beers was still fun, but being out there amongst it was much better. Another stint playing cricket in England seemed the best way to keep my cricket career going. Obviously the dream was to play for Australia but I never really thought about it seriously because I had never taken playing cricket that seriously. It wasn't a job or a career to me. It was just something that I liked doing.

The tour to Zimbabwe, in August 1991, was the next step in a long learning experience. The captain was Mark Taylor and there were two other Test players in the side, Steve Waugh and Tom Moody. A former Test player, John Benaud, was manager. He was also a Test selector at the time. Things were getting serious.

I spent most of my time on that tour with Steve Waugh and we've been close mates ever since. I'd met his younger brother Dean in England that winter and talking about Dean with Steve in Zimbabwe helped us to get to know each other. Steve impressed me a lot. He was very professional. He knew how to work at his game but also how to relax when the time was right. Steve helped me out on that tour, trying to show me what was going on and how the whole thing worked.

On a Dakota, somewhere above Zimbabwe, heading for a day out at Victoria Falls. It was the tour where Steve Waugh and I became close mates.

It was my friendship with Steve that led to the idea that I move to Sydney and try to play for New South Wales. I knew Steve and Dean well and the SCG pitch was a turner. At that stage Victoria had Paul Jackson and Peter McIntyre and myself as the spinners. 'Macca' and I had been on the tour to Zimbabwe together and had both bowled pretty well. But I'd been dropped by Victoria towards the end of the previous season so the idea of moving north and hopefully bowling on a spinner's pitch appealed to me. At one stage I even told the Waughs I was coming. But the idea certainly didn't appeal to a few of my Victorian teammates.

Before the start of the 1991–2 season, the Victorian squad had a trial game at the Albert Ground. Simon O'Donnell's XI played Dean Jones's XI and by then everyone there had heard that I had been approached to move to New South Wales. At first Deano didn't say anything to me, but the coach Les Stillman came over for a chat before the game.

"Deano just said something to me you might find interesting," Stillman said. "He said that if Warnie is thinking about going somewhere else to play, tell him we don't want him to play here. Tell him to piss off. If he doesn't want to be a Victorian we don't want him playing in our trial games. Someone else can play."

Deano certainly made me think about what I was going to do. Then Simon O'Donnell said, "Listen mate, there comes a stage in your life when you've got to back yourself to play. You're good enough. If you're prepared to put the hard work and the time in and believe in yourself you will play for Victoria. If you really want to do it you will."

They were all pretty aggressive with me and at the time I didn't like it too much. I'd only played one Shield game at this stage and didn't expect all this fuss, but I look back on it now and I realise it helped me at an important time in my career. Eventually Les told me I had half an hour to decide what I wanted to do. I asked for an hour, then went for a walk around the ground. One of my best mates, Darren Berry, had a word to me. He said that it was a good opportunity for me to play for New South Wales with the Waughs and Mark Taylor and bowl on the Sydney pitch and that I had to give it serious thought. But he also said that what Deano, Les and Simon had said was worth thinking about. Did I really want to give up my hopes of playing for Victoria and move to live in another city? I thought hard about it and realised I wasn't ready to give up and move interstate. I liked living in Melbourne — still do — and when the heat was put on me I knew I couldn't do it.

"I'm not going," I finally told them. "I'll stay and try to play for Victoria."

It was the right decision, I think. I had an interesting and similar incident at the start of last season, my first as Victorian captain. Matthew Elliott had a big offer to go to South Australia and I had to advise him on what I thought was the best thing for him.

"Look mate," I said. "How many South Australians are playing in the Australian Test side? None. Well, can you think of a reason why? Not really? Well, for starters they are playing at Adelaide Oval where the perception is that it is a good pitch and short boundaries square mean it has a reputation for easier runs. A thousand runs at the Adelaide Oval are not as good as 800 at the MCG where the outfield is slow and there is more in the wicket."

I said to Matty, "Look, if you want to play for Australia you have to weigh up what is best for you. You have to be comfortable with whatever decision you make. And whatever decision you make is the right decision, you have got to believe it is the right decision. I can guarantee you your time will come. You are a good enough player and a good enough bloke and your time for Australia will come if you are prepared to do the hard work. The other thing is, I don't think the ACB likes blokes who change states all the time. Just keep that in the back of your mind."

Matty decided to stay, although the offer would have tripled his income from Shield cricket. I was happy with the decision I made, but at the time it was a pretty tough decision to make. The ambition of any bloke playing Shield cricket is to play for Australia. It has to be. You can go and work somewhere and make a good living, earn twice as much as you will earn playing Shield cricket. But if you love cricket as much as we all do, it is hard to give it away. It's too much of a challenge, for a start. The trouble is that these days you can't just love cricket and play because you'll go broke. You won't be able to have a family unless you and your wife are both working and, if you are, you'll never see each other. Bills, a mortgage, a car, a phone, power — you can't pay all those bills on a Shield wage. That is unless you have a very good employer who will give you time off and that's rare.

So it was a pretty big decision for Matty to make. He took his chance, worked amazingly hard through the off-season, made two big scores when it really counted and then made his Test debut in Brisbane in the First Test against the West Indies in November 1996. The knee injury from that collision with Mark Waugh in the Second Test, when Matty was 78 and looked to be cruising to his first Test hundred, was a tragedy for him and the Australian team. But he worked hard again and came back just as good a player in a tough series against South Africa. Once you've had a taste of Test cricket you want to have more, to really test yourself and your ability in the best cricket in the world. I think Matthew Elliott is a good enough opening batsman to play a lot of good cricket for Australia.

I came home from Zimbabwe and started playing for Victoria straight up at the start of 1991–2. I played the first three games and then was chosen to play for Australia against India in the Third Test at the SCG. From being this chubby young bloke who just loved having a beer and a good time and playing some cricket with his mates, I was about to represent my country, to become only the 350th person to play Test cricket for Australia. It had never been a dream or a goal of mine to play for Australia. All I wanted to do was play Aussie Rules footy, but that ambition eventually changed once the importance and the privilege of playing for Australia hit home. Out of every single person who has ever played cricket in the world, only 349 had played for Australia and I had somehow joined that group as Number 350. Not many is it? It is a great privilege, although it took a while for me to fully realise that I had to make the most of the opportunity I'd been given.

Although I was new to top level cricket, I had at least been overseas a few times. I was no great scholar at school but I was reasonably street smart. I was 18 when I first went to Europe with a few mates, then I had played in England in 1989 and 1991. I'd learned about street life a little I suppose: things like passports, money, pickpockets, what really goes on out there and how to survive. But the world of the Australian cricket team was vastly different. The way I found out about my selection and the way I reacted probably tells something about where I was at that stage of my life.

My old mate from our time in league cricket in England, Dean Waugh, came down to Melbourne for the Second Test against India. Naturally enough we enjoyed ourselves socially. We spent a couple of days at the Test, having a few beers in the Members Pavilion. I remember standing there with beer and pie in hand watching the cricket with Dean, Brendan McArdle, Warren Whiteside and a few other Melbourne district players when Australian team coach Bob Simpson and manager Ian McDonald walked past.

"G'day guys," I said.

"You set for the day, Shane?" they asked.

"Bloody oath," I replied. "I got me pies, me beer and everything here."

I had a lot to learn.

On the last day of the game, we were back in the Members but in a slightly different context. The news was out that I'd been chosen to replace Peter Taylor in the next Test in Sydney.

STEVE SIEWERT/THE FAIRFAX PHOTO LIBRARY

A photo taken at the SCG nets in November, 1991. I'm preparing for a
Sheffield Shield match against New South Wales, the old enemy. I didn't
know it, but I was on the doorstep of the Australian Test team.

"Hey, here's Shane Warne," Dean was telling people. "He's going to play in the next Test." There we were, a pie with sauce in one hand and a beer in the other and all the Members wondering what was going on. We couldn't stop laughing.

That evening Ian McDonald rang to say, "Shane, congratulations. You have been picked for Australia. Can you come down to the Board office in the morning?"

I immediately rang my family and some mates and told them what was going on. I invited them to a small party on at my parents' place that night. We celebrated hard and I was suffering the next morning.

My father had to drive me to the ACB office as I was not up to scratch first thing that morning. As a family we'd always liked nice cars and that day Dad dropped me off in his Porsche. There were cameras and media everywhere and they must have thought I was a real poser, getting dropped off in a Porsche. Still, I had other things on my mind — a hangover.

I remember telling Graham Halbish that I was nervous and a bit queasy and that if he could hold off the media for a while I'd appreciate it. I headed straight for the safety of the toilet but didn't quite make it in time.

Somehow I got through that ordeal and the next day I was in Sydney, at the Old Sydney Parkroyal in The Rocks, meeting up with my new team-mates, many of whom I hadn't met. I'd met Allan Border once at a Prime Minister's XI game. I knew Mark Taylor from the Zimbabwe tour and Ian Healy from the Australian XI games. I'd met David Boon once. Apart from Merv and Deano, whom I knew well from Victoria, I didn't know Geoff Marsh, Greg Matthews, Mike Whitney or Bruce Reid.

It was a strange experience coming into such a high profile team with all these big name players around I didn't really know. At least I'd been meeting players from interstate and overseas during the previous year or so through the Academy and the tours to the West Indies and Zimbabwe.

On December 31, New Year's Eve 1991, two days before the Test, Boonie and 'Swampy' Marsh looked after me. We took a few beers — quite a few — up to the roof of the hotel to watch the fireworks on the harbour and see in the New Year. It was a fine gesture from two experienced players. They were taking me under their wings and introducing me to the whole scene. It ended up being a pretty big night. Welcome to the Australian cricket team, Warnie.

If Swampy thought he had done his duty as far as I was concerned on New Year's Eve, he was wrong. On the first morning of the match I was nervous and unsure what to do. Should I take my whole kit across to the nets for the hit-up before play? Or only the basics, my bat, pads etc? I was watching what other guys were doing, but I needed some personal assistance. I happened to be next to Swampy in the dressingroom.

"Swamp, can I follow you around today? Do you mind? I've got no idea what's going on."

He was happy to help and so ended up with S Warne a metre behind him for the rest of the day.

From memory I weighed about 95 kilos back then. My diet was not too flash and I still have to battle the urge to tuck into a hamburger or a toasted cheese sanger. At the tea break on the first day of the Test, the room attendants brought in all these party pies and sausage rolls. They don't provide that sort of food for us any more — unfortunately. But that day I didn't hesitate. I scoffed right into them before the team physiotherapist, Errol Alcott, came up to me.

"Shane, I don't think you need any of them."

"No, it's okay Errol, they're great," I replied.

"Shane, you don't need them. You're in the Australian team now and you need to lose weight."

When the food came out for the tea break the next day, I did the right thing and did not touch a pie or a sausage roll. After a few minutes I heard a whisper. It was Swampy quietly handing me a little parcel wrapped in white tissue paper. I could see a little spot of red seeping through the top of the paper wrapper as he passed it to me. I can truthfully say that that party pie never passed my lips.

That first Test was an amazing experience. Someone who never thought he would play for Victoria was suddenly playing for Australia, facing Kapil Dev out in the middle of the Sydney Cricket Ground. When my brother Jason and I used to pick our backyard teams one of us would pretend to be Kapil Dev, Garth LeRoux, Viv Richards, Allan Border or David Gower. We used to have to bat and bowl like them, to imitate their style.

It did not seem that long ago since I'd been playing those games in the backyard. Now I'm in the middle of the SCG facing the great Kapil Dev with a Test match in the balance. There were 15 minutes to go. Bruce Reid was injured and I wasn't sure whether he was going to bat. Everyone else was out besides Allan Border and me.

India had fieldsmen all around the bat chattering away with Kapil and Manoj Prabhakar bowling. The crowd was roaring and I had the legendary AB at the other end performing one of his last rescue missions for Australia. I was wondering what I should do and who was going to help me and AB was yelling at me, "This is a f.....g Test match here. Come on, dig in. Don't get out."

I could not help wondering just how I ended up in this situation. A week before I'd been with Dean Waugh and a few of the district lads drinking beers at the MCG and watching a Test match from a safe distance. But I did try to make the most of the experience. I've always been observant of people and how they react to different situations. And my eyes stayed wide open during that first Test to everything that was going on even though most of it was new and some of it went straight over the top of my head.

We managed to hang on and save that game, but not before Ravi Shastri had had his fun with me, especially after I dropped him off my own bowling when he was on 66. He went on to make 206 and Sachin Tendulkar a brilliant 148. I took 1/150 off 45 overs. I was in the big time alright.

The next Test was in Adelaide and by the start of the fifth day Australia was in a position to bowl out India and win the game. That morning before we began our warm-up, Bob Simpson called us together and told us Swampy and Mark Waugh had been dropped. Everyone was stunned and the warm-up and fielding practice before play were pretty ordinary. By the time we were about to take the field, AB had told us he was not coming out for the start. Paul Reiffel was 12th man and in his laidback way was about to have a shower at about 10 to 11 when AB asked him what he thought he was doing, then told him to get his whites on. 'Pistol' made the mistake of asking why.

"Because I bloody said so!" AB said.

That was the fastest I've ever seen Pistol move.

As Swampy Marsh led us onto the field, AB was on the phone to Laurie Sawle, chairman of selectors, demanding that the decision to drop those two be reversed, or a good reason be given. AB did not get what he wanted, but he did take the field and led us to a good win. Afterwards we packed our bags to leave that night and AB told us he was not coming.

"I might see you in Perth," he said. As we left we weren't really sure whether he was going to come over to Perth for the Fifth Test or resign. It is history that he did arrive a day late and carried on as captain, but he was not a happy man. It was an amazing way to start an important day's play in a Test — and it was only my second. Test cricket was certainly dramatic stuff.

At the Academy

A lot has been written and spoken about my time at the Cricket Academy in Adelaide and about the reasons why I left in some controversy. The Academy is such a high-profile and successful part of the Australian cricket set-up that it is important I set the record straight about my time there.

Personally, without doubt the best thing to come out of my time at the Cricket Academy in Adelaide was meeting Terry Jenner. Terry, or 'TJ' as he is known in the cricket world, is not only a close mate but also the best spin bowling coach I've come across. He has been a great influence and support throughout my career and I'll talk more about him in later pages. Apart from meeting TJ, the two other major things I gained from the Academy were learning the routine of regular training and how to bowl a flipper from head coach Jack Potter.

The Academy was still in its early days when I arrived in April 1990 and I suppose there were bound to be teething problems. At first I put in well at training. I was keen and worked really hard, but the atmosphere and some of the attitudes of the people running it at the time began to get to me and I ended up turning off. It was a shame but my laidback approach did not go down too well.

A couple of examples might give you an idea of what the Academy could be like in its early days. Put a group of fit and healthy young blokes together for a few months of hard training and there will be times when they want to let off steam. We were no different. Most days we would be going somewhere around Adelaide in a minibus — to early morning swimming sessions or net sessions later in the day. On those trips we often took the idea of letting off steam pretty literally by mucking around farting. Eventually they started fining us for farting in the bus. The year before they had even sent Martin McCague to the doctor to have his bowels checked. You can imagine how well that went down with the boys in the bus.

We used to go swimming once a week, starting at about 7 in the morning, usually on Fridays. The trouble was that Thursday nights were pretty lively in Adelaide and I often used to go out all night. At one stage I'd forgotten my goggles two weeks in a row. The third week I had a big night out and stayed at a mate's place overnight. I woke up at about 5.30 and realised it was too early to ring TJ for a lift. So I booked a taxi then rang my mate at the Academy, Damien Martyn (who is still one of my best mates), and asked him if he would mind driving my car to the pool and bringing my swimming gear, including my goggles. The plan was for me and Damien to get there first and to be changed and ready to go before anyone spotted that I hadn't been home that night. No such luck, of course. As I got out of the taxi there was Peter Spence, Jack Potter's assistant, 10 minutes early. My hair was standing on end, I smelt of alcohol and I still had my jeans and shirt on from the night before.

"Oh, g'day Spencie," I said, trying to look full of beans. "I forgot some of my gear and had to go back and get it."

"Yeah, sure Shane."

Damien had brought some of my stuff but forgotten my goggles. This time Spence gave me some Speedos but made me swim the whole session without goggles. The pool was heavily chlorinated and after about three or four laps my eyes started to burn badly. We've all been in those pools. After that session my eyes were really sore for quite a while.

Even though I did not enjoy a lot of the Academy routines, there were only a few things I refused point blank to do. I would not go for a run or a jog after a day's play. We'd worked hard all day in the field and were then expected to go for a run instead of sitting in the dressingroom having a beer and a chat about cricket, which is just as important as running or lifting weights. But the all-time classic was when the AIS wanted to test how much body fluid we'd lost during a day in the field or a long training session. We had to go into the dressingroom, squat down and, with the help of some KY Jelly, stick a gadget up our backsides and leave it there while we went back to the nets for more batting and bowling. After that we had to plug it into a machine which would give a reading on how much body fluid we'd lost that day.

Sorry, guys. There was no way I was going to do that. Instead, when no one was looking, I'd duck into a toilet and tape the gadget inside my shorts and later I'd ask one of the other players what reading he'd got.

"Thirty-one? Ah right."

Then later I'd volunteer, "Thirty-two for me today, guys."

ABOVE & RIGHT:
A few of the major influences on my life,
my Mum Brigitte and Dad Keith, and Jack
Potter — the 'flipper' is mostly his.

SAM CHESHIRE/THE ADVERTISER

LEFT:
Peter Spence,
Cricket Academy coach.

Of course all that made me feel a little out of place at the Academy.

Then when the team to tour Sri Lanka later that year was chosen I was left out. I was considered a liability, too much trouble to take on tour. So while the boys went off to Sri Lanka I stayed in Adelaide, doing the Academy's version of solitary confinement.

It was chaos that whole year. There had been problems between Potter and Spence. Finally Jack told Spence that one of them had to go. Spence said he was not leaving so Jack announced he was resigning. Then a week later Spence resigned and we were left without a coach. Eventually Andrew Sincock and Barry Causby, two former South Australian Shield players, took over the Academy on a temporary basis.

Throughout that year some students lived at a pub and others at St Mark's College. Somehow they'd put me in the pub at Port Adelaide. We weren't allowed to drink in our hotel, but we could go up the road and drink in the next pub. We ended up having a really good relationship with the owner of the hotel we were living in. He had no problems with us. Steve Cotterell and I used to have a few beers at the pub and we got to know the locals pretty well, blokes from the Port Adelaide football and cricket clubs. Spending some time with those guys was good fun, but finally the time by myself at the Academy began to drive me crazy. After a week or so of trying to train on my own — which was not exactly inspiring — I was told to go to South Australian state squad training. I went a couple of times but still felt out of place. I remember bowling to David Hookes in the nets. If I bowled one outside his leg stump he'd hit it by swinging his bat behind his back then say, "Don't bowl there son." I just shut up and kept bowling, but I wasn't enjoying it much.

After a week or two Jim Higgs, Victoria's Test selector and a former leg-spinner, rang me to see how I was going. I told him the truth and he just suggested I hang in there for a while, and if it's still not working in a few weeks, then come back. And that is what I tried to do, even though all I really wanted was to go home and train with the Victorian squad. Apart from Jack Potter's help with the flipper and Terry Jenner's friendship and coaching, I had not received that much encouragement as a young leg-spinner. Leggies had not been fashionable for quite a while with a lot of people. Around this time Les Stillman, the former Victorian player and South Australian coach who had moved back to Melbourne to coach the Victorian Shield team, said in the press that there was no longer any role in first-class cricket for spin bowling. Tim May and I often thought of that statement when we were taking wickets in Tests for Australia a couple years later.

MARK RAY

BEN RADFORD/ALL SPORT

I'm hard to find in the top photo. The occasion was the match
between England and the Cricket Academy at St Peter's College, Adelaide,
in 1990. I'm on the right shoulder of Robin Smith, the England batsman,
who is in the second row from the front, third from the left. In 1993 I
became something of a 'monkey on his back'. In the front row, fourth from
the right, is Graham Gooch, England's captain. In 1993 I got him at
Lord's, caught by Ian Healy.

Anyway, there I was in Adelaide, the only student at the whole Academy, learning very little and wondering why I wasn't back home in Melbourne. Then one day I was watching a game at the Adelaide Oval in a box with Murray Sargent and a couple of the other SA selectors and they told me they were thinking of picking me for the next Shield game, which was in Sydney. At that stage Academy players from interstate could be chosen to play for South Australia. Michael Bevan made a century on Shield debut, but for South Australia not New South Wales. Eventually the other states objected so strongly that the system was changed and the Academy players no longer stayed in Adelaide for the whole summer. In the end, the SA selectors decided against picking me, but that business helped me make up my mind.

The next day I wrote a letter saying that I had come over to the Academy to try to improve my skills. Okay, I stuffed up once and did the wrong thing. I'd been a bit of a pain. I knew that and I'd been punished. I'd lost my allowance and a tour to Sri Lanka, but I did not see any point in staying in Adelaide on my own. I told them I thought I'd be better off back home in Melbourne training with the Victorian squad and trying to break into that team. And that is what I did. I put the letter in an envelope, left it at the Academy office, packed my gear in my white, six-cylinder Cortina with big extractors and mag wheels, pulled back the sun roof, turned up the stereo full bore and headed east to Melbourne. Bye, bye Academy.

Two weeks later I played my first game for Victoria, against Western Australia at the Junction Oval. And one of my best mates at the Academy, Damien Martyn, was in their side.

Marto and I have been through a fair bit together. We were close at the Academy and we both liked a good time. No prizes for guessing that that did not sit well with the officials. Then later, as well as starting our Shield careers at about the same time, Marto and I started playing Test cricket at the same time, and we ended up sharing a lot of intense experiences. We were the first two young blokes — 21- or 22-year-old guys, the next generation — who started playing Test cricket in the early 1990s. That was the time when players like Bruce Reid, Geoff Marsh, Greg Matthews, Dean Jones and Michael Whitney ended their Test careers. Marto and I still keep in touch as often as possible and hopefully we'll play more Test matches together. He's a very gifted player.

Marto and Justin Langer were pretty close at the Academy. They looked alike and because they were both from WA they trained a lot together too and the rest of us spotted this. When you are living that close to guys and training hard with them things can occasionally become a little heated. I remember one day in the nets Stephen Cotterell became frustrated bowling to Justin and after one delivery said to him, "Mate, the only difference between you and Damien Martyn is that you think you can play, but Marto can play." Justin lifted his bat and headed towards Stephen. It became a bit heated, but all was okay. They weren't laughing but the rest of us were.

JACK ATLEY/THE AGE

Damien Fleming and the West Indian opening batsman Sherwin Campbell share a joke during the 1997 tour to Australia. It was a friendship that had begun on an Australian Youth tour to the Caribbean half a dozen years before.

Another time Marto, Justin and I were mucking around in my room, a bit of wrestling and whatever. I went in and helped Marto out at one stage and ended up getting Justin in a headlock. He is a black belt in a form of kick boxing. I was roughing him up and giving him little annoying punches in the head and telling him to either do something or give up. I was still holding him when he said he'd give up, but then he jumped up and smacked me in the nose. Justin always had determination and fight about him and he was always keen to learn. That is why I've always liked him.

Experiences like those strengthen friendships and were good things to come out of my time at the Academy.

When I look back now at those days at the Academy, I have no doubt that the best thing was meeting Terry Jenner. The next was learning to bowl a flipper and the third to train properly. But I don't think I learnt too much about cricket there besides the flipper that Jack Potter taught me.

At one stage at St Kilda, Shaun Graf asked Jim Higgs to come down to a net session and show me how to bowl a flipper. It was tough going at first. Whenever I tried one the ball went everywhere, over the batsman's head, into the side netting, all over the shop, and because of the slight change in action required to bowl the flipper, I lost my leg-break for a while. I was still struggling with it at the Academy, but Jack helped me get through. At one stage he told me I had too many things going on in my head. Instead of just running in and bowling I was thinking about all these different things and confusing myself.

"Don't think about too much," he said. "You know how to work batsmen out; you know how to bowl various deliveries, so just do it."

Then Jack put a piece of paper the size of a plate on a good length, put a blindfold on me and told me to bowl a leg-break. I bowled it perfectly first ball.

"Get rid of all your thoughts and just bowl." That was a valuable lesson, one I try to apply even in the middle of a Test match when the pressure is on.

Jack was mainly a batsman, but he did bowl leggies and he knew a lot about it. He would show me different ways to bowl deliveries and my flipper is a mixture of his and Jim Higgs's. But mostly it is Jack's and I'm very grateful to him for that and all his other help.

In those early days the Academy was having teething problems, but even so some very good players came out of our troubled year: Damien Martyn, Justin Langer, Greg Blewett, and Jason Gallian. The point about the Academy is that the players can already play the game by the time they are chosen to go there. The Academy is there to fine-tune them. What the Academy

The graduates. Damien Martyn and I shared time at the Cricket Academy and the MCG victory over the West Indies in the 1992 Boxing Day Test. Our skipper was Allan Border.

does, especially now Rod Marsh is running it, is to bring in people like Dennis Lillee, the Chappells, all the great Australian players, to teach the young guys how to improve in specific areas. Dennis teaches the fast bowlers, Ian Chappell helps the batsmen with their hook shot, with playing spinners or with their slips fielding. Rod gets baseballers in to teach them how to throw. The thing is that the Academy students are learning from great players, people who've been through it all, who've learnt the hard way, who know the problems and ways to fix them. That is why it works so well nowadays. It's great for people to do a level three coaching course and pass on that knowledge, but the best young players need to learn from the best, from people who've been through the same experiences and worked their way through the same problems. Still, young players have to work some things out for themselves. As Ian Chappell always says, they have to know themselves first.

Then there is Rod Marsh. He is brilliant at improving players' confidence and getting them to play the game in an attacking way. As well, they learn everything from stretching to the psychology of the game, how to prepare for a match, how to regulate their diet (I would have struggled with that course I reckon), how to train properly on the weight circuits to improve their strength in the right areas for their particular game. Rod also teaches them how to celebrate a big win and how to sit around and chat with past players, opponents and each other about the game just as he did when he was playing.

The strength of the Academy now is the access it has to past players and their knowledge and experience. And a strength of Australian cricket is that those past players are prepared to share their knowledge. That was one thing Geoff Marsh emphasised when he took over as Australian team coach. As he said, if someone has a problem hooking he will get Ian Chappell in; if Mark Taylor has a slips catching problem we will get Bob Simpson or Ian Chappell in to have a look at him. If I've got a problem Terry Jenner will drop in or if Mark Waugh is having trouble with his new off-spinners 'Swampy' might get Ashley Mallett in for a session. 'Swampy' has no hesitation with that because he knows that his role as a coach is to oversee what is happening in the Australian cricket team and to help each player to develop and improve. That's how he sees his role as team coach and that is how Rod sees his role at the Academy.

I don't think that happens in England, for example. England has often used former county cricketers who only played a handful of Tests with no great success. They need people like Ian Botham, Allan Lamb, Robin Smith, David Gower, Graham Gooch. If they know that Australia is going to bring Shane Warne and Michael Bevan to England for the Ashes then they have to look around for the best player of spinners in recent times and get him in to advise the current batsmen. That is the way we do it in Australia, and I suspect the way that most other countries are going about their development is wrong. The news that England's new coach, David Lloyd, has brought Botham in to advise the bowlers and generally be around the team is a step in the right direction.

That leads me to one of my few gripes about the Academy. I don't think they should be inviting players from other countries. They have had young players from Pakistan and New Zealand in for special coaching and I don't see why we should do that. The established countries should look after their own. We can advise them on how we run our Academy but let's not bring their young players to Adelaide. Instead we could go up to Darwin or Alice Springs, out to the outback to look for talent there. There has to be plenty of it, given the way Aboriginal kids play football. When I went to Soweto with Jonty Rhodes we saw tremendous talent in the black townships. Some of those kids will be playing for South Africa in five or 10 years' time.

The only other thing that worries me about the Academy is that some of the players leave it thinking they should walk into the Test team. Really all they've done by that stage is played against a couple of Second XI sides and maybe a senior touring team. Because they have been on some overseas tours they think that they are ready, that they are better than they really are. That is not to say the new young guy in a Shield team should have to mind his Ps and Qs like he had to in the past. He does not have to be treated like a servant or be the last one in the showers each night. I am glad those days are gone. Everyone should be treated with respect, but that includes the older guys who have been around for a while and proven they are good enough to survive. The young bloke who comes into the side has not done much yet and he has to earn his stripes, earn respect. An example of the right way to do things is signing your autograph on a bat. I was always taught if you only just started playing you signed down the bottom. A lot of the young guys these days just grab it and sign up near the captain's signature. You should earn your way up the autograph bat. I think the guys out of the Academy sometimes lack respect for the players who have been around for a while.

When I first came out of the Academy, I don't think I was arrogant. If you are going to go to the top in your sport, you have to have confidence in your own ability, but there is a difference between confidence and arrogance. Viv Richards had an aura and an arrogance about him; so did Allan Border, but they weren't stuck-up people. AB was as down to earth as you will find. He loved his beer and his chats with the boys. But AB had done it all and he had earned enormous respect. He'd won that respect the hard way. Maybe no one has had a tougher time in his early days, especially his early days as Australian captain. I just think some of the Academy players need to understand that first-class cricket is quite tough. Nothing comes easy and they have to earn respect out in the middle by playing well consistently. Sometimes the academy blokes think they don't make mistakes and are not prepared to listen. The only way to learn is to listen, to make mistakes but to learn from them. If you don't take that approach then you will not know how to react when you start struggling. And every cricketer struggles at some stage. It's the one who battles through who makes it in the long term. And anyone who goes to the Academy should remember that for every Academy graduate who has gone on to a good first-class career, there have been plenty who have not made it at all.

They are my few criticisms of the Academy as it operates now. Otherwise I think it is fantastic. I enjoy going back there each year for the spinners week. I enjoy helping younger cricketers as well as just meeting them and swapping stories. I'm not one to hide my knowledge. You only get knowledge from the experience of playing. I had played 52 Tests prior to the tour of England and about 100 first-class games so I have got a fair bit of experience and I'm happy to pass on anything I've learned to the next generation. It's part of my responsibility as an Australian cricketer — and it's a lot of fun as well.

There's a lot more to life than cricket. With Simone on our wedding day, Melbourne, September 1, 1995.

THIS PAGE & OPPOSITE:
Winners are grinners.
Anticlockwise from
above – in the tickertape
parade through Sydney,
acknowledging our
winning back of the
Frank Worrell Trophy in
the Caribbean in 1995;
after beating Australia
A in the World Series;
and, two magic
moments in our back-
from-the-dead win over
the West Indies in the
1996 World Cup semi-
final. But behind all the
smiles there was pain –
my spinning finger was
wearing out.

Back to my best! It's the vital First Test against South Africa in Jo'burg, 1997, and the batsman is my old 'bunny' Darryl Cullinan. Out for a duck.

Two family snaps, front row, second from the left in both,
and I'm just a boy with a dream – all I wanted to do was play footy
with St Kilda. But I was too slow ... I turned my hand to cricket,
the other sport I'd always played.

OPPOSITE:
Howzat for size? My first Test cap was against India at the SCG
in 1992. I got one wicket, Ravi Shastri, for 150 runs.

ABOVE & RIGHT:
The team. The
names and faces
might change,
however little, but
we always know
how to celebrate
a win – and that
includes quietly!

PREVIOUS PAGE:
Sometimes I found
myself in at the
deep end during
my time at the
Australian Institute
of Sport's Cricket
Academy in
Adelaide.

**Rodney Marsh, now
the Head Coach at
the Academy, has
the knack of offering
invaluable advice and,
at the same time,
generating confidence.**

CLIVE MASON/ALL SPORT

**I reached the crossroads - if I was going to get going in
cricket then I had to get tough on myself.**

"I tried the 'flipper' ... it just came out of the hand perfectly."
The end of Richie Richardson at the MCG in the 1992-93 series was
the start of the great turnaround in my career.

A son in the limelight, and a father in the background. The happy family moment followed my match-winning effort against the West Indies in the MCG Test. Thanks 'Moe' (Greg Mathews).

SHAUN BOTTERILL/ALL SPORT

ABOVE & OPPOSITE:
Time changes just about everything – except the demands a
bowler makes on an umpire for a favourable outcome.

OVERPAGE:
The Ashes tour is **THE** tour, but sometimes even its magic
can get a little wintry.

Now or Never

In my first two Tests, against India in 1991–2, I finished with figures of 68-9-228-1, an average of 228. When I finished that season as 12th man for Victoria in our last Shield game in Melbourne against Queensland the summer ended on a disappointing note. At the time the Victorian team seemed to be ruled by the medium-pacer mentality. The ruling theory then was that you had to be a batsman, a fast bowler or a medium pacer who could also bat. Spin bowling was very much out of fashion in Victoria and it was hardly a surprise that the spinner who did play in that final Shield game for Victoria, left-arm orthodox Paul Jackson, soon moved to Queensland. Victoria's number one leg-spinner at that stage, Peter McIntyre, followed Jackson's example and moved to South Australia. Both moves paid off. Jacko played in Queensland's two Sheffield Shield winning finals and Macca not only played in SA's Shield-winning team in 1995–6, but he also won selection in the Test side through his success with South Australia.

The next series for Australia was in Sri Lanka in August and September 1992, about five months after the end of our season. I'd needed to finish the season off well to have a chance of going to Sri Lanka, so to end it as Victoria's 12th man made me think I had no chance of making that tour. That realisation made me think a lot about what had happened that summer, going from Shield cricket to Test cricket and back again. I'd had a taste of international cricket and, like everyone who experiences that honour, I wanted more. So I set about assessing my whole game.

I asked myself where I needed to improve to return to the Australian team. I analysed my whole game and worked out what I needed to do to become a better player. I needed to improve my batting, my general fielding by becoming more flexible and agile and my catching by hard practice; I needed to gain more variety with my bowling and to increase my confidence in my bowling. Perhaps the most important question I had to ask myself was what was the weakest part of my game. If I was to be honest —

and there was no point kidding myself because anyone who does that will not survive at the top level — there was only one answer: my fitness. By the end of that season I weighed 95 kilos. When I played footy and ever since I'd left school I'd been 84 or 85 kilos. I had never been fat. But since my first trip to England in '89 I'd been carrying weight and when I got back from there in '91 I was huge. Too many pints and too many pies.

There was only one thing to do if I was to play for Australia again, even for Victoria. I needed to make some sacrifices. So every morning my alarm clock would go off at 7am, I'd get up and go for a run then to the gym or to the pool, sometimes all three. I did that six mornings a week for four months — on my own. I had Sundays off. I got my weight down to 82 kilos, losing 13 kilos in about four months. I went off fatty foods, off alcohol, off everything that would stop me from reaching full fitness. All I wanted to do was play for Australia. I kept telling myself that was all I wanted to do and that everything I was going to do would have to work towards me playing for Australia. During that off-season I also went back to the Academy in Adelaide to work with Terry Jenner and Rod Marsh. I spoke to Jim Higgs, Bob Paulsen, the former Queensland and Western Australia leg-spinner and, of course, Richie Benaud, whom I'd first met in England in 1991.

During that winter, Merv Hughes had gone into hospital for a groin operation and one night Tony Dodemaide and I went in to see him. Dodders and I said we had no chance of making the tour to Sri Lanka. Merv suggested we bet a dozen Crown Lagers and whoever missed the tour would have to buy the guys who were chosen a dozen. Although at that stage it seemed that Merv had the best chance of the three of us, we agreed to the bet. We must have been feeling sorry for the patient.

Dodders and I roomed together in Sri Lanka and we'd often ring Merv in the middle of the night.

"G'day big fella, how ya going over there, mate? Not too cold is it?"

It was usually about 3am in Melbourne and Merv and his wife Sue didn't take too kindly to it. It was lucky that we were all good friends.

The key event for me on the tour to Sri Lanka was the last day of the First Test — or really the night before when Greg Matthews boosted my flagging confidence. In the first innings I took 0/107 off 22 overs to take my Test career stats to 1/335. So there I was. I'd done all this hard work during the winter to get myself as fit as possible and I'd sought advice from plenty of experts but I still couldn't take a wicket. The evidence was hard to ignore: it seemed I was not good enough to take wickets at Test level. I was fit, but I just was not good enough.

Australia made 256 in the first innings and Sri Lanka 8/547 in theirs. In that second innings we fought hard and got to 471, a lead of 180. In our second innings most of the top order got decent scores before Greg Matthews made 64 at number 7, Craig McDermott 40 and myself 35 in 98 minutes. Mike Whitney and I batted for 37 minutes for the last wicket partnership, adding 40 valuable runs to take our lead up to 180. That 35 and the 24 I made in the first innings, improved my confidence a little as I felt I'd contributed something, even if I was there mainly to take wickets, not make runs.

On the night of the fourth day, Greg Matthews ran into me in the hotel lobby and asked what I was doing for a feed. He suggested we go across to the Hilton Hotel for an Italian meal. 'Moie' knew I was down and he was going to try to lift me. He has always been a good mate to me throughout my career but his support and advice in this Test match was invaluable.

"Man," Moie said over a plate of pasta, "they wouldn't have picked you if they didn't think you could bowl. So stop getting up yourself. 'Suicide', you and I will do it tomorrow and we could be bowling for Australia for the next five years. So let's go and get them tomorrow. Don't worry if they bounce twice. Go out there and spin them as far as you can. You'll be right.

Greg Matthews offered me invaluable support: "Mate," he once said, "they wouldn't have picked you if they didn't think you could bowl."

If you bowl well these blokes won't be able to play you."

Moie called me 'Suicide' because I was blond and a song around at that time was 'Suicide Blonde' by INXS. His encouragement helped. By the time we got back to our hotel I was raring to go. I went to bed but had a restless night's sleep. I knew I had to do something the next day otherwise I was just about gone as a Test cricketer.

We batted on for a little while that fifth morning and eventually left them 181 to win, not many but enough to give us a chance. I came on to bowl just before lunch and my first over went for 11 runs. Allan Border took me off. He had to be careful as he didn't have many runs to play with. Sri Lanka got to 2/127, 54 to win. At one stage Aravinda de Silva hit Craig McDermott over mid-on and AB dived but just missed the catch. It seemed like it was not going to be our day. Then Aravinda did the same in Craig's next over and this time AB threw off his hat and his sunglasses, ran back past mid-on, dived and took an absolute screamer. It was a great captain's effort, a brilliant catch and typical of the way AB could inspire his team. We were still in with a chance if we could apply some pressure.

Mo was bowling very well at one end and eventually AB threw me the ball. We needed four wickets and they needed less than 30 to win. I was really nervous. The way I'd been going the match could have been finished in one over. I thought they would just belt me and finish it off quickly. Mo was at short cover, not far away from me, giving me support in his unique way. "Come on Suicide," he was calling. "Spin 'em hard. Spin 'em up, Suicide. Let's go, Suicide."

I bowled a maiden first up and gathered some confidence. They were landing where I wanted them to land. Moie took a wicket next over and I started thinking we were a chance. Then next over I took a wicket — my first for the match. Deano ran over and said, "Well done, mate. You're only averaging 160 now." The situation was really tense and Deano was just trying to relax everyone. I tried to laugh, but couldn't. I was too nervous. Next up Moie bowled a good over and I took another wicket in my next. "Now you only average 80, Warnie," Deano said. By this stage we needed one wicket to win and they still needed 25 runs. Then came another two boundaries off Mo and things were very tight.

Asanka Gurusinha had made 137 in the first innings and was still in at this stage. He went for a sweep shot off Mo, missed but Ian Healy could not make the stumping. Next over Madurasinghe hit me to cover, in the air straight to Moie and we'd won the Test match. It was mayhem after that. It was AB's first win as captain on the subcontinent after years of trying.

Sri Lanka had lost 8/37 and somehow I'd taken 3/0 off 13 balls. Moie finished with 4/76 and 7/169 for the game plus 6 and 64 with the bat.

If that Test had been on television in Australia it would be remembered as one of the great matches of all time. It was a brilliant finish and the locals could not believe how we had won, let alone how we celebrated in the dressingroom. In fact I wish I could remember every little thing that happened on that tour. Moie was tremendous. He took wickets and seemed to make 50 in every innings. Heals had a great tour and then in the last two Tests, Mark Waugh made four ducks.

At our games in Colombo we had a great bloke as our room attendant. His name was Sirripala. Sirry was tiny, about 5 foot, had no teeth and was a great little guy. He used to leave the ground each evening on our bus and then in the middle of the city, with thousands of people everywhere, he'd jump off and hop on a bus with people already hanging off the doors. This was all new to me and it was an amazing experience to see how these people lived. All his life Sirry had been saving for a tiny block of land on which to build a house for himself, his wife and their two kids. It would have cost him something like $1000 but it was a lot of money to him. At the end of the last match, after Mark Waugh had made his fourth consecutive duck, he called Sirry over and said, "Sirry, you can have my bat, my gloves, my coffin, my shoes, my whites. Everything. They're no good to me." Then the rest of us got together all the money we had on us, put it into a couple of plastic bags and gave it to him. Sirry was overwhelmed and started crying. His dream of buying that land and building that house for his family had come true.

Those three wickets changed things for me too. I missed the Second Test with a foot injury and did not take a wicket in the Third, which was rain affected, but at least I'd done something constructive in a great victory, a victory that gave us the series 1–0 and gave AB his only series win on the subcontinent.

Back in Australia I started the 1992–3 Shield season fairly well but I was dropped again for the First Test against the West Indies. I was still very fit and training hard so it was a major disappointment. I still hadn't secured a regular spot in the Test side even though Australia was playing the West Indies, who were supposed to be vulnerable to leg-spin. Australia failed to bowl out the West Indies on the last day of the First Test in Brisbane after dominating most of the game. After the match, Allan Border said in the press that "if we had Shane Warne in the team, I reckon we could have knocked them over". This was a huge boost to my flagging confidence. I thought then that if I could maintain form in Shield games I might get back in the Test side soon. When you learn that the captain wants you in the team and is prepared to say so publicly, you have to be close to selection. Soon after that, in a Shield game against Western Australia at the Junction Oval, my club ground, I took 5/49, 2/74 and scored 69 with the bat. Soon after I was chosen for the Melbourne Test, starting on Boxing Day.

In the first innings of that Test I took 1/65, made no runs and was feeling the pressure again. By the start of the fifth day, the West Indies needed 327 to win off 90 overs with nine wickets in hand. I woke up that morning thinking, "Today's the day. I have to do something good today or I'm finished." It's amazing the thoughts that go through your head when you're under pressure. The papers were saying the same thing, that the game situation was made for me — a fifth day pitch, a decent target to be chased. The line in the papers was "This is Shane Warne's last chance to show what he is made of. He has played seven Tests for five wickets with an average of 90. He has not done much at Test level. He is on his home ground and he will be bowling on a worn pitch."

I had to agree with that view. The situation was perfect for a leg-spinner, the sort of situation which leg-spinners are chosen to exploit. With about half an hour left before lunch, the West Indies were cruising. They had not lost a wicket, Phil Simmons was smashing us and captain Richie Richardson was playing very well. It looked like they were going to get the runs and win the Test. I tried a flipper to Richie and it just came out of the hand perfectly. He did not pick it, went back — which is what you want when you bowl a flipper — and was bowled as the ball kept a little low on the fifth-day pitch. From 1/143 they were all out for 219 and we had won by 139 runs. I finished with 7/52 and ended the day feeling much better than when I began it. All that practice with Jack Potter at the Academy trying to get the flipper right had paid off in one delivery, a delivery that might well have saved my Test career, a delivery that certainly turned things around for me. Looking back now I can say definitely that that ball was the turning point in my career.

Mo Matthews was 12th man in that game and after the win he ran out into the crowd and grabbed my father and brought him into the dressing-room. Beer was being sprayed everywhere. Dad just kept in the background, watching quietly, but it was a special moment for both of us. And a very thoughtful gesture from Moie, another example of the support he'd shown me over those few difficult months. A lot of people, including me sometimes, think Mo goes too far at times, but I'll always have a soft spot for

Richie Richardson after being 'flippered' at the **MCG**. He might have been thinking, "What happened there?", the same thought that was to cross Mike Gatting's mind six months later in an Ashes Test at Old Trafford.

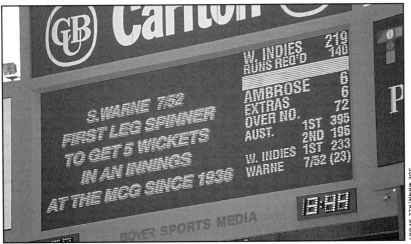

The message on the **MCG** scoreboard gave me a real buzz.

him because of the generous support he gave me when I really needed it.

After that great victory in Melbourne, which gave us a 1–0 lead, the West Indies fought back well. Brian Lara made the most of a flat pitch and a damp ball to make a great 277 in Sydney in the next Test, we lost in Adelaide by a run and Curtly Ambrose wiped us out in Perth for the West Indies to snatch the series 2–1after being down 0–1. It was a savage blow to lose that series, but it taught me a lot about Test cricket, about how tough and challenging it is, but also that I could perform with the ball at that level. That last lesson was what I needed badly after the previous series in India and that frustrating but ultimately encouraging series in Sri Lanka. After the Fifth Test in Perth we left for three Tests in New Zealand. I played in all of them and, with my confidence improving all the time, bowled pretty well. I ended with 17 wickets at 15.06, a new record for Australia in New Zealand. An Ashes tour was coming up in a couple of weeks and, although Australian leg-spinners had not done very well in England for years, I was confident of being selected. An amazing year was about to be followed by the dream tour, an Ashes tour. I was about to go back to England not as a young bloke bumming around and playing some cricket, but as an Australian cricketer on the most famous tour of all. My career had come a fair way from those lonely early winter mornings pounding the roads in Melbourne and that plate of pasta in Colombo with Mo Matthews.

Balls of Fire

The one ball I've bowled which has received the most attention — the leg-break that bowled Mike Gatting in the First Test at Old Trafford in 1993 — was probably as great a moment as I've experienced. Yet a well planned dismissal can be equally satisfying. When you have worked hard on a batsman, tested his technique with various deliveries, finally worked out the best way of getting him out and then produced the right ball and taken the wicket, you can be fully satisfied. Still, any Test wicket makes you happy and when it is a player of the calibre of Mike Gatting, you have to be very pleased. Yet in many ways I'm still not sure exactly how I managed to produce that ball as my first in Test cricket in England.

England's softer, slower and lower pitches have not helped Australia's long list of leg-spinners, so I knew I would have to land the ball well on the 1993 tour to be successful. If a spinner drops short on English pitches, he will get belted. Length is crucial. With the record of previous visiting leg-spinners in mind, I was a little worried when Graeme Hick attacked me in the lead-up game against Worcester. Allan Border had told me not to show him too much variation, just bowl mainly leg breaks. He was going to be in the England Test team and AB did not want me to show too much before the series started. But a bowler has pride and no one likes getting smashed around the park. Basically, I stuck to what AB told me to do but the hammering from Hick was not much fun.

A few weeks later there I am in the middle of Old Trafford in my first Test on English soil. I'd watched the series in '89 while on my first visit to England and imagined myself playing for Australia in a series in England, as every young Australian cricketer does. But to actually be there and be in the team was still a thrill. At times you have to pinch yourself. We made 289 in our first innings which was not bad but not as good as we'd hoped after our openers, Mark Taylor and Michael Slater, had put on 128 for the first wicket. England's new off-spinner Peter Such had taken six wickets in the innings and that gave me some encouragement. Some of the press had suggested that the England bosses had made sure Old Trafford would be a spinner's pitch because they thought their spinners, Such and Phil Tufnell, were much better bowlers than Tim May and myself. Maysie was not chosen for this match, but I was confident that if I bowled well I would receive some help from the pitch. In Hick, Gatting and Graham Gooch England had three batsmen widely recognised as very good players of spin bowling. The scene was set for an interesting contest.

So the call from AB comes: "Warnie, you're on next over."

I don't do a heavy warm-up, a few loosening swings of the shoulders and a few stretches of the arm and fingers. It takes me about an over and a half to really feel loose and fully into my action, but for some reason I've always been able to land my first few balls fairly accurately. Some spinners start with a few innocuous deliveries just to get into a rhythm. I usually start with my stock ball, the leg-break, and I usually try to spin it fairly hard. That's the way I bowl so that's the way I start. With the ball to Gatting all I tried to do was pitch on about leg stump and spin it a fair way. As it left my hand it felt just about perfect. When a leg-break works really well it curves away to the leg-side in the air before pitching and spinning back the other way. The curve in the air comes from the amount of spin on the ball and in this case I had managed to put quite a lot of purchase on this delivery. That is why it dipped and curved away so far and then spun back such a long way. I knew I'd bowled Gatt and I could tell from the look on Ian Healy's face behind the stumps that the ball had done something special, but it was not until I saw a replay during the lunch break that I fully realised just how much it had done.

After stumps that day the England players came into our dressingroom for a drink and Gatt just looked up at me and said, "Bloody hell, Warnie. What happened?"

I didn't have much of an answer for him.

"Sorry, mate. Bad luck."

Then we both laughed. There was nothing more either of us could think to say. It was just that sort of dismissal.

I suppose that ball was the perfect leg-break, pitching outside leg-stump and hitting the top of off. Any bowler would be happy with that although I was just as happy with the ball in the next over that had Robin Smith caught by Mark Taylor at slip. But it was the Gatting ball which attracted all the attention. For the rest of that tour — and that dismissal happened in the first of six Tests — hundreds of people asked me about that ball —

ALL SPORT

Two views of **THAT** ball. On the
right, is the way just about every
English cricket fan saw it on the
back page of their newspapers
the morning after.
Above, is my view of the magic
moment. 'Gatt' looks a little stunned,
but we shared a laugh about it later.

whether I planned it, whether I did that sort of thing all the time, how I did it, what grip I used, how did I spin the ball that far — every question you could imagine. I gave them the same answer I gave to Gatt. "Dunno really. I got lucky."

The press got very excited too. One newspaper offered me £25,000 to pose in the nets wearing only a jock strap. The fax machines in the hotels were working overtime. The whole thing was getting out of hand. The press liked the idea of me being a beer-swilling beach bum who had been turfed out of the Cricket Academy. I seemed to be their idea of your typical Aussie rebel.

On the day I got a little carried away myself. After dismissing Smith I thought I was in for the perfect day and tried too hard to take wickets. Eventually I calmed down and from then I bowled well and had a good series. "Warnie," Heals said, "you've already got the master covered after two Tests." I found out later that Richie Benaud's best series in England, in 1961, brought him 15 wickets in the four Tests he played. As well, my 34 wickets in a series in England passed Clarrie Grimmet's record for an Australian leg-spinner of 29 in five Tests in 1930 and Bill O'Reilly's 28 in five in 1934. Those figures were as amazing to me as the ball that bowled Gatt.

Perhaps one of the more satisfying dismissals on that tour came in the second innings of that First Test. The thing about the Gatting ball was that it came from nowhere — a great thrill but not quite as satisfying as setting up a good batsman, working a tactic out to counter his technique then bowling the right ball to get him out. That is what happened in the second innings when I had Alec Stewart caught behind. Alec had been pushing forward to me but keeping his bat close and sometimes half behind his front pad. The leg-break was turning so he refused to follow it, preferring to keep his bat tight in close near his leg and allow the leg-break to spin past. I also tried wrong'uns and toppies but Alec was able to cover them with his pads as well. It was a fair enough tactic but it was frustrating for me. You want the batsman to use his bat, even in defence. No bowler likes seeing good balls passing the bat untouched.

So what to do? The zooter is one ball I bowl that not many people really understand. Basically it looks like a leg-break when it leaves the hand, but the difference is that it floats out of the front of the fingers with some back-spin on it. The batsman expects the zooter to turn but instead it often floats through to him fairly harmlessly and then goes straight on off the pitch. It sometimes dies on pitching too whereas the top spinner, which also usually goes straight through, tends to dip in the air and jump off the pitch. The zooter tends not to do much at all, but that can be just as dangerous as a ball that does a lot.

Sometimes a small variation is all you need to trick a batsman.

The plan with Alec was to continue giving him leg-breaks and let him keep letting them go, then to slip in a zooter and hope that he doesn't pick it or that it was not spinning sideways through the air like a leggie. In that case the ball might just take the edge of the bat on the way through. And that is exactly what happened. The zooter pitched on a length just outside off stump. Alec pushed forward again and kept his bat in close to his knee expecting another leg-break to spin past him harmlessly. But this time the zooter kept its line, clipped the edge on the way through and Ian Healy took a wonderful low catch. If you ever see the video of that dismissal you'll see a big reaction from me and that was because a plan had worked. The ball might have looked like a nothing ball but that was exactly what it was supposed to look like — to Alec Stewart and I suppose to anybody else.

Alec Stewart was on the receiving end of another of my favourite balls in the next Ashes series, this time in Brisbane in the First Test in 1994–5. We set England 508 to win in the fourth innings and Alec and Mike Atherton had reached 50 for the opening stand when I bowled to Alec, who had made 33 of that 50. I'd just given him a short ball which he cut for 4. Occasionally I'll do that on purpose to set up a batsman for the flipper, but hopefully that short ball gets hit straight to a fielder. All batsmen love hitting a 4 and their confidence usually grows after a good shot. Sometimes they can forget that you have dangerous deliveries up your sleeve. They become just a little complacent and that's when you can deliver a killer blow. I thought that the next time Alec saw a short one coming he might get onto the back foot quickly and look for another boundary. They had started well and if they could get on top of me in my first spell they would be travelling pretty well. Luckily for me the next short one was the flipper and it landed perfectly. Alec didn't pick it and he lifted his bat high for another cut shot, but this time the ball did not turn away to the off to give him room to cut but landed much fuller than he expected then skidded straight on to bowl him. It was as good a flipper as I've bowled and it finished off a planned dismissal very nicely.

Bowling Graham Gooch behind his legs in the second innings of the Fifth Test at Edgbaston was another planned dismissal. I'd noticed that Gooch, who generally played me very well, occasionally just poked his left leg out past the line of leg stump when I bowled wide. I thought at times he was a little casual doing this and the night before I told Allan Border that I reckoned I might bowl around the wicket to Gooch and try to sneak a slightly fuller deliver behind his legs. AB liked the idea and we were absolutely delighted when it worked.

I suppose one ball that caused a fair amount of discussion was the one that bowled Basit Ali between his legs in the Sydney Test in 1995–6. Basit was pretty cocky that summer and had been telling me and Steve Waugh, who was usually fielding in close when I was bowling, that he was the next Javed Miandad. Sadly I never enjoyed the great challenge of bowling to Javed but I know enough about him to know he was a great player and enough about Basit to know he was not. So with one ball of the day's play to go on the Saturday evening and Basit on 14 and Pakistan 3/101, we needed to try something, anything. I glanced down the pitch at Ian Healy and he glanced at me. We both thought that a midwicket conference was the way to keep Basit under pressure a little longer and to make him think we were hatching some mysterious plan.

"What are you doing for dinner tonight?" Heals asked me.

"Dunno," I said. "What d'ya reckon about the last ball? I've got to make him play at it not pad it away."

"Flipper?"

"Nah, a leggie I reckon."

"Jeez, it'd be funny if you bowled him around his legs," Heals said before walking back to the stumps.

So I walked slowly back to my mark and came in and let rip a big leg-break. It spun from wide of leg-stump and Basit tried to push it away with his left leg. But he left a gap between his legs and amazingly the ball went straight through it and bowled him. We were all stunned. Heals and I could not resist the temptation to do a little myth-making by saying we had planned to bowl Basit between his legs. Heals told one journalist that story after play and I wrote that in my column in the *Sunday Age*. In the end Steve Waugh wrote in a magazine that we had made up the story and there was some controversy about it all. We were never trying to deceive the public or take a lend of the media. Basically we were trying to have a little fun, but it backfired on us. The main point was that I'd bowled Basit, the next Javed, through his legs. It must have embarrassed him no end and it certainly gave us a lot of laughs. Really it was another ball like Gatt's ball, a big leg-break that took off and did something special, but it wasn't planned.

Of course, for every plan that works and every ball that does something out of the ordinary, there are plenty that don't do what you want. They might not be obvious but they happen regularly. Twice I've been on hat tricks and not bowled a good ball. The first time was to Phil Tufnell in Brisbane in 1994–5 and the second to Jayantha Silva in the Test against Sri Lanka in Melbourne in 1995–6. Both times, with a rabbit on strike, I bowled wide of the stumps. In fact, on that second occasion I remember turning towards the crowd in the outer after the ball passed through to Heals and putting both hands around my neck. I'd choked.

The hat trick I did manage, against England in Melbourne in 1994–5, was a mixture of planned and unplanned balls. The first, to Phil de Freitas, was supposed to be a big leg-break which hurried straight through rather than turning and trapped him leg before. The second, to Darren Gough, was another big leg-break which, this time, did turn a fair way. Goughie tends to push out in defence, so I fancied my chances of finding the outside edge if I landed it on a length. It worked and he was caught behind. Then to Devon Malcolm it was either death or glory for both of us. Devon either slogs or blocks, nothing in between, so I thought I'd bowl a big over-spinner which would either spin a little either way or go straight through. It was David Boon's birthday that day and as Devon came out I remembered missing Tufnell in Brisbane and realised that this time I had to make sure the ball was on the stumps. The rest was up to Devon. As Devon faced up, my mum and dad were watching up in the stands with Shaun Graf, who predicted confidently that this time I'd get it right and take my first Test hat trick. He was right. In the end Devon pushed forward to block and the ball went straight on like a top spinner. It bounced a little, took his glove and lobbed wide of Boonie who dived to take a great catch.

The Victorian Cricket Association gave me a framed print of the next day's *Age* with photographs of the three dismissals and the match report. That and a photograph of the Gatting ball have pride of place on a wall next to my pool table at home in Melbourne. Special moments, and let's hope they're not the last ones; let's hope it keeps happening. Please.

Trouble in the Bull Ring

Only a half an hour or so after the Australian team landed in Johannesburg early one warm February morning in 1994 we saw something from the bus taking us to our hotel that seemed like a bad omen for the rest of the tour. People were heading off to work all over the place, walking across fields, queueing for buses, packed into the back of pick-up trucks. And in the middle of all of this there, on both sides of the freeway, were about six bodies with white sheets draped over them, victims of a car accident. It was quite a shock. Welcome to South Africa.

There had been a lot of people at the airport to welcome us, plenty of media and a few hundred fans. For so many people to be there at 6 o'clock in the morning showed us right away that Australia's first tour to South Africa for nearly 30 years was big news. The attention and the hype did not let up.

At that stage we had no idea how things would deteriorate over the next month. We expected a bit of flak from some people because there had been a few controversies during the series against South Africa at home which had just finished. The television cameras had shown me having a few words to Darryl Cullinan in a couple of games and our umpires had been accused of giving some crucial hometown decisions, especially in the Third Test in Adelaide, which we won to draw that series 1–1. But on that first morning in Johannesburg, we had no idea how tough the tour would be.

There have been some difficult times in my life and my sporting career, but that tour to South Africa was definitely one of the most difficult. By the end of the First Test, back in Johannesburg I had been fined $1000 by the ICC referee for abusing Andrew Hudson and then copped an extra $4000 fine from the Australian Cricket Board. And back home people everywhere, including David Hookes and ABC Radio's Tim Lane, were saying Merv Hughes, who also got fined the same amount, and I should be sent home. The reason Hookes and Lane gave was that Australia had lost the First Test with me and Merv so they wondered how much the team really needed us. It is a great honour to represent your country so it is a real shock to find out that back home you are being described as a national disgrace. I am the first to admit I did the wrong thing that Sunday in Johannesburg. I deserved the ICC fine and accepted it at the time, but it took me quite a while to restore my reputation, to prove that success had not gone to my head. Although I accept the blame for stepping over the line, a little background might just help to explain what happened on that tour.

During the tour there was a lot of hype about whether this was Allan Border's last tour. He'd said publicly that he would not decide about retirement until after this tour, but obviously it was on his mind a lot while we were in South Africa. I wish he was still playing. Dean Jones ended the tour by announcing his retirement, so he was obviously feeling frustrated. He did not play a Test and was eventually dropped for the last one-dayer. A lot was happening inside and outside the team. We were under pressure in a number of ways. It was that sort of tour.

From the moment we got off the plane at Johannesburg we seemed to be in the spotlight. Not that we weren't in the spotlight in Australia, but in South Africa the attention was more intense and in-your-face. Everywhere we went people wanted to meet us, to touch us or get our autographs. And, at the risk of appearing to be pumping up my own tyres, I seemed to be the centre of a lot of the attention. As Ian Healy has said in his book, it was as if Elvis had risen from the dead. A lot of that attention was pleasant and I always had the impression that people respected me for my bowling. I enjoyed making new friends, but in Johannesburg during that First Test there was also a lot of aggro in the attention and it got to all of us. It was the aggressive attitude of the public which really got up our noses. And it turned out that I let it get to me and eventually I blew a fuse in a big way.

I hope I've never refused to sign an autograph for a kid unless I had good reason, but I don't like it when kids' parents are rude. In South Africa at times I found that parents did not ask for an autograph for their children, they demanded one. Often in the lobby of our hotel they'd corner me and say, "Hey Warne, sign this for my kid." Many of them were very rude and they would push and shove each other and us to get what they wanted. And often they did not even bother to thank us. After a while we got sick of this and tried to ignore the rude people. But it was a no-win situation because if we refused to sign we would have disappointed a kid and the parents would then accuse us of being "stuck-up Aussies".

I remember Steve Waugh trying to have a hit-up down on the fence after stumps one day during the Test and people hassling him to come over and sign their books or bats.

"Waugh, sign this man!"

No "please" at all. A few times Steve asked them to wait five minutes until he'd had his hit, but they were not prepared to wait. In the end he walked over to the fence and told the people that unless they stopped annoying him he wouldn't sign anything.

Although there was supposed to be plenty of security at our hotel, a few people got through and banged on our doors in the middle of the night. You'd wake up with a start and think it was the manager trying to get you up because you'd slept in. I also received lots of phone calls, many wishing me good luck and a good tour but also many that were abusive. In the middle of the night a call would come through. I'd wake up and hear some guy on the other end say, "We'll get you today, Warne! We'll f...ing get you today, you Aussie ....!"

This was in the middle of a Test match and it was not too reassuring to know I might be fielding on the boundary later that day, maybe only a few metres from that caller.

The Johannesburg ground is known as the Wanderers, but unofficially as the Bull Ring because of the aggressive attitude of the crowd. Ian Redpath had his cap pulled off his head and thrown away as he walked down the Wanderers race one day on the 1966–7 tour. We were not the first team to cop it over there. It's a long walk down to the ground and the fences on either side are not that tall. As well as yelling abuse at us, people used to reach over and grab us as we jogged down onto the field.

The Bull Ring – Wanderers ground in Johannesburg.
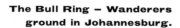

They'd knock your hat off or grab your shirt and pull you up against the fence. By the time we got through that race and onto the field we were spoiling for a fight. In fact it was Steve Waugh, normally a cool, calm character, who said that it was only a couple of weeks later that he realised he'd never felt so angry during a Test match as he had at Johannesburg. All of us felt like that. No visiting team should have to put up with that sort of abuse. In fact their officials should look at changing that race to protect the players.

On the Sunday, the fourth day, Australia was in a bit of trouble in the match and morale was not so much low as very fragile. I fielded on the

CLIVE MASON/ALL SPORT

fence for most of the first session and as usual tried to have some fun with the crowd. After all, they are the people who keep the game going and who love it as much as the players. Someone would yell out, "Warne, show us your mystery ball," and I'd peek down my trousers. Or someone else would tell me to pull up my pants and I'd walk around with them hitched up as far as I could get them. All good fun, but then there'd be a nasty comment. I was struggling to understand that crowd. One minute we'd be having some fun together and then it would turn really aggressive. At one stage someone threw an orange and hit me in the middle of the back. I looked across at the security guards who were squatting down near the fence and were supposed to be protecting us and they were laughing.

Allan Border had decided not to bowl me until about the 44th over. I was down there fielding and wondering when I was going to come on to bowl. Andrew Hudson and Hansie Cronje were going well. Things were slipping away from us a little. Eventually AB came up and said, "We need you Warnie. Come on, get us a wicket."

After all the trouble back at the hotel and at the ground, by the time I got the ball for my first over I was really pumped. I was in a state and wanted to show all 40,000 people at the ground that I was going to fix them right up. I was desperate to get a wicket and with my third ball I bowled Hudson behind his legs. That set me off. I lost it completely and started telling him to "F... off. Go on Hudson, f... off out of here!"

Andrew Hudson is a good player and a lovely bloke, a good friend of my close mate Jonty Rhodes. Andrew had done nothing to deserve that sort of abuse. Eventually Ian Healy grabbed me and tried to stop me. I look back at it now and wonder what was going on. The film of that incident is pretty awful and the guy in the footage is not the real me. Later Paul Reiffel and David Boon said they had noticed that I was angry even before the game. Paul, who was 12th man, said I had been rude to him when I asked him to get a few balls so I could have a warm-up bowl one morning. Boonie said I seemed angry and tense for the whole week. "You weren't yourself. You're normally calm and happy-go-lucky," he said. "Is everything alright at home?"

After play I had to front the ICC match refereee, Donald Carr. Allan Border and the manager Cam Battersby went with me. We all knew I'd done the wrong thing and we accepted the $1000 fine Carr imposed. On our way from Carr's room to our dressingroom we had to pass by the South Africans' rooms. I saw Andrew Hudson and apologised to him straight away. I told him there was nothing personal in it and he was fine. In fact most of

MARK RAY

Black day in the Bull Ring, 1994. Merv Hughes tries to reason with an abusive fan in the players' race, while his fellow batsman Tim May takes cover. Merv's aggression cost him a hefty fine.

the South Africans just had a good laugh about it all. They had no problems with me, which was a relief as the teams had been getting on very well.

What really upset the Australian players was that later the ACB fined Merv and me an extra $4000 with no right of appeal. To us this seemed unfair. We'd already been fined by the ICC referee who, at first, was not even going to fine Merv at all. In the end he was swayed by how bad Merv's sledging looked on television. The ACB's Graham Halbish and Alan Crompton had come over and they imposed the extra fine, but they never spoke to us or asked for our side of the story. I thought it was very bad that Alan could fine us when he wasn't even there. Sure, Merv and I lost our tempers, but the ACB never allowed us to explain the poor behaviour we'd had to handle every time we travelled up and down that race.

It seemed the pressure from the media back home left the ACB with no choice. I was furious when I heard that Tim Lane had said on ABC Radio that he was "ashamed to be an Australian" and that Derryn Hinch on the Midday Show said that what I had done was an absolute disgrace. Hinch said that I obviously had no mind of my own and that I just did whatever Merv did. Hinch said he had met me and Simone at the 1993 Grand Final and had liked us, but that a year later I had obviously got carried away with all the success and publicity. Then I heard that David Hookes had asked whether the team needed Hughes and Warne over in South Africa at all. He said Australia had lost the Test with us so why keep us over there. I was really disappointed in those reactions, especially in Hookes's comments because he was an aggressive cricketer who always had plenty to say on the field. These people were making up their minds and making big statements from thousands of miles away. They did not know what was going on behind the scenes. I can tell you that I don't respond too well to requests for interviews from those three guys.

By the end of that Test match the whole thing had become a major controversy. The team had gone up to Sun City, north of Johannesburg, and the media followed us up there. Merv and I had a round of golf with the rest of the team and we had television crews hassling us all the time. With all this going on, it got to the stage where it was the Australian team against the world. Whenever the pressures develop like that and the team feels it has been hard done by, the seige mentality tends to take over. After Sun City we travelled to our next match, a three-dayer against Boland at Stellenbosch, a beautiful wine-growing district outside Cape Town which Merv christened "Still on the Booze".

Mark Taylor had a chat to me on the team bus during the Boland game, just to see how I was and to ask what was bugging me. All the players knew I was not myself, but their support and a few words from my father who had arrived on a pre-arranged trip certainly helped. Dad did not make a big fuss and his advice was mainly for me to put the controversy behind me and get on with the rest of the tour.

That support helped me personally, but even so the whole team was still upset at the ACB fines and felt that Merv and I had been made scapegoats. It finally got to the stage where we had a meeting in Allan Border's room and talked about boycotting the next tour game against Boland in Stellenbosch. AB was angry and thought that the ACB had made the decision to fine us without knowing the pressures we were under. They obviously were not listening to our manager Cam Battersby.

In the end we realised we could not boycott a tour match. We had to show we were bigger than that. And we did that in the Second Test at Cape Town which we won to square the series 1–1. Unfortunately that was Merv's last Test match.

Looking back at that tour a few years later, I still cannot really explain exactly why I blew up like that. It must have been a combination of factors. We were at the end of a long summer of three Tests against New Zealand

and three at home against South Africa. I was probably feeling a bit worn out from all the travel and the hassles with some of the people in South Africa just sent me over the edge. As well, some of the success I'd enjoyed might have made me big-headed for a while.

Australian cricketers these days are paid well and, as a professional cricketer, we have to handle the public pressures that come with the baggy green cap. I accept that. I know you cannot have it both ways. But we all make mistakes under pressure. A boss in an office might blow up and abuse his secretary, but no one knows about it because it happens in private. When an Australian cricketer blows up it is often in public and everyone sees it. We cannot avoid the television cameras. They help pay our wage and bring the game to the people, but there are times out on the field when emotions get the better of you and you forget that a few million people might be watching. International cricket is a tough game and unless you're emotionally committed you won't survive. I suppose the main point about what I did on that tour is that I think I've learned from it and I am a more mature person for the experience. In particular, I hope I'm more aware of how an Australian Test player is a role model for thousands of young people.

Learning from a tough experience usually comes at a cost and that tour was no different. One example: a close school mate of mine was due to get married around that time and I was to be best man. As it turned out the wedding clashed with the tour to South Africa and I had to miss it. That was disapppointing, but what was worse was that I was in such a state during the tour I did not even send a message or a fax to wish him well. We are not as close now and have lost touch with each other, which is a real shame. And another lesson I suppose.

Despite all the difficulties I have many great memories of that tour. Most people were fantastic, very supportive and encouraging. I received lots of letters from South Africa after I came home to Melbourne and almost every one was sympathetic, people saying how much they had enjoyed watching me play and that they hoped I'd come back soon. I replied to all of them and sent each person a little gift, a signed photograph or something. But on the tour there were enough troublemakers to make life very difficult. It was a sort of love/hate relationship. At times I experienced more hostility than I had in any series although, once again, I admit I did the wrong thing.

Some of the best memories from that tour were the enthusiastic kids I met at the coaching clinics I did with Jonty Rhodes in some of the townships. In the first few days of the tour the Australian team went out to Soweto and it was a deeply moving experience. Their cricket ground was not much

MIKE HEWIT / ALL SPORT

more than a paddock by our standards and they did not have much equip-
ment. I had never seen anything like it and was pretty upset. What chance
would these kids have of playing cricket for the new South Africa? And
facilities matter so much in a cricketer's development. During the 1995 tour
to the West Indies Justin Langer asked Jimmy Adams why their players did
not dive to save the ball. He gave two reasons: one was a general attitude
that said that a good shot hit through a gap deserves 4; the other that as
kids West Indians play on rough fields where you'd injure yourself if you

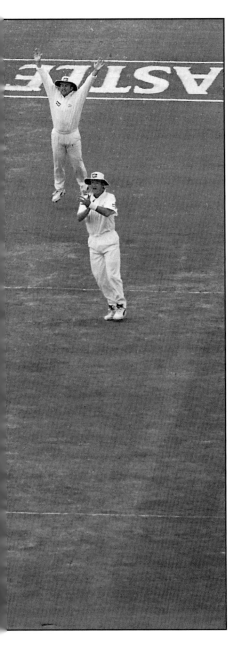

Magic moment in the Bull Ring, 1997. I get one through the defences of Gary Kirsten.

dived for every wide ball in the field. In other words, the facilities did not encourage diving so they did not learn that skill. It was a fascinating glimpse into another cricket culture and really made me think about those things.

In South Africa in 1997, the public were fine. That aggressive minority had calmed down a lot and we had no problems. In fact, after my experiences in 1994, I was asked to address a team meeting before the First Test in 1997 to explain to the players who had not been to Johannesburg before, and to remind the others who had, what they might expect from the crowd. At least I was putting my past mistakes to good use.

Unfortunately our travelling and training schedule was so tight that I had few opportunities to go into the black townships for coaching clinics as I had with Jonty Rhodes in 1994. Back then Jonty had agreed to do clinics in the townships for the sponsors, Baker's, a biscuit-making company. Jonty is really popular in South Africa and a devoted Christian. After seeing Soweto I told him that if he wanted me to come along I would as often as our schedule allowed. At times we went into areas where a white person on his own would have been in great danger. But the reponse we received was tremendous. Sometimes there would be 5000 people there — kids, parents and onlookers. It was not easy working out a way to coach that many kids so often we grabbed a microphone and just talked to them about our lives and our cricket. The enthusiasm of those kids made me realise how lucky I was to be earning a good living playing the game around the world. Hopefully one day before I retire, a young South African opponent will come up to me during a Test match and tell me he was at one of those clinic backs in 1994.

Malik and Me

Some of the worst months of my life were those that followed the revelations that Salim Malik had offered Mark Waugh, Tim May and myself huge sums of money to play badly in Pakistan in 1994. I was stunned when I left Malik's hotel room to think he was serious about having $200,000 there for me in half an hour if I agreed to bowl badly. And I was worried by the affair for the whole of the 1994–5 Australian season.

Mark Waugh knew Malik from their days at Essex in English county cricket. He didn't know Malik that well, but certainly better than the rest of the Australian team. Malik seemed a little distant to me. The Pakistanis come from such a different culture that it is often hard to get to know them, especially the ones who do not speak English that well. Malik's English was fine as he'd had those years at Essex, but he always seemed aloof, not one you'd feel comfortable approaching in the dressingroom after a day's play.

My only substantial contact with Malik before that tour was in the middle and he was certainly one of the best batsmen in the game. He played me very well and he used to have plenty to say while he was batting. And I said my share back to him.

I enjoyed bowling to him because he presented a challenge. He was cocky, had good footwork and read the flight and spin better than most. Like most Pakistanis he was a wristy player which meant he could alter his shot late and use his wrist work to place the ball through gaps. A difficult customer for any spin bowler.

The basics of the bribery affair are well known — how Malik, then Pakistan's captain, approached Mark and myself at a function and said that he would have $200,000 for us and a couple of other players if we played badly in the one-day game which was to be played the next day. Then on the fourth night of the First Test Malik rang my hotel room and asked me to come and see him in his. He was wearing one of those long white robes that are traditional dress in Pakistan. He kept telling me that Pakistan could

SHAUN BOTTERILL/ALL SPORT

**Salim Malik and me, during the Third Test at the SCG in 1995.
The bribery business on Australia's previous tour to Pakistan
left me stunned.**

not lose. When I asked him what he meant, he said again, "You don't understand. We cannot lose."

I told him Australia was going to go out the next day and beat Pakistan.

"No, you don't understand. We cannot lose. I am saying to you, you and Tim May are the two key bowlers tomorrow. There will be $200,000 cash in your room in half an hour if you don't bowl well tomorrow. Bowl outside off stump and it will be a draw."

I was stunned. Was he serious? That is big money to be able to supply on the spot. I told him I'd get back to him then I returned to my room. I was sharing with Tim May.

"What did The Rat want?" Maysie asked. We had called Malik 'The Rat' for quite a while because he had a long face. I told Maysie and his reaction was typical tongue-in-cheek Tim May stuff.

"Hmmm, $200,000 eh? Half an hour eh?"

Then Maysie started laughing and told me to ring Malik and tell him we were going to beat Pakistan the next day. As the record books show, Inzamam-ul-Haq, with one wicket left and 3 to win, came down the wicket and tried to swing me over midwicket. He missed, but so did Ian Healy. The ball went for four byes and Pakistan won a great, but to us very disappointing, Test match. Afterwards, Malik told me I was stupid because we'd lost and I could've have had the money. He made more approaches during the rest of the one-day series.

Things might not have looked good early on that last day of the Test when Tim May was on and off the field with strained neck and Glenn McGrath with a strained quadricep. With Craig McDermott already out of the game with a foot injury, Joe Angel and I were the only two fit front-line bowlers. Joe and I busted our guts for Australia that day and as it turned out I ended with 5/89, but unfortunately the result went against us.

As we all know, the bribery business has never been resolved. A Pakistani judge would say his report ended the matter and in a way it did because nothing further has happened. But that judge also called Mark, Tim and myself liars for making the accusation.

Firstly we did not just blurt out the story to the first journalist we met in the hotel lobby. We reported it to our captain Mark Taylor who reported it to coach Bob Simpson and manager Col Egar. That sort of thing is too big for two or three players. And once the officials became involved it was out of our hands. Secondly we are not liars. Why would anyone make such serious allegations knowing they were false? Inventing something like that would cause more trouble for us than for the accused. In fact Malik did threaten to sue the Melbourne *Age* for being the first newspaper to name him as the person who made the bribery attempt. As far as I know he has not gone ahead with any legal action. Why not? If the judge was right and we were lying why didn't Malik sue us and the *Age*? He'd have made a fortune out of the case.

I am not wealthy, but with some good management I shouldn't struggle for a quid for the rest of my life. Touch wood, anyway. So I wouldn't make that story up for monetary reasons. I don't understand why anyone would think I would invent the whole thing. What have we got to gain by making it up? Nothing. Malik thought of a reason, of course. He reckoned I made the accusation to upset his batting as I was struggling against him. That is just the way the Pakistanis think. They have a completely different lifestyle to us. Besides, I'm happy to back my bowling against anyone and if Salim Malik or any other player is too good on the day, good luck to them. That's the game.

As Mark, Tim and I said two weeks before the First Test against Pakistan in Australia, we told the truth and we stand by the statements we gave to the Australian Cricket Board. We were hoping that would be the end of it and we could concentrate on the return Test series. We were certainly not going to Pakistan to attend that judge's inquiry. The whole betting scene in India and Pakistan is illegal so the people running the betting are basically gangsters. Not the sort of people to trust or to play around with. Who knows what might have happened to us had we gone over for the inquiry? If the International Cricket Council had launched an inquiry in London we would have gone, but not to Pakistan.

Playing against the Pakistanis or watching their scores from overseas in the papers is now a strange experience. They are such a talented team that whenever they collapse for a low score or bowl badly and are beaten you cannot help wondering about what might be going on behind the scenes. Hopefully nothing, but it is difficult not to wonder sometimes.

It was certainly very satisfying to beat them 2–1 in the home Test series which followed our visit there. The month or so leading to that series was an awful time. The judge handed down his report, Malik had arrived on his own a week or so after the rest of the team and at that stage we did not know what the authorities would do. I felt under tremendous pressure and although advised for legal reasons to keep quiet I eventually felt compelled to defend myself in my column in *The Sunday Age*. Tim May also felt that way and the same week put out a statement to try to stop the rumours and counter the judge's accusation that we had invented the whole story.

I'm a cricketer not a lawyer so it was a relief to finally get out on the Gabba in Brisbane and start the series. When I dismissed Malik for a duck in the second innings I felt justice had been done, at least to some extent.

The bottom line in this affair is that you cannot prove anything. Legally, it is our word against his. There were no video cameras hidden in his room like there were in the Grobelaar soccer bribery scandal in England. A few Pakistani players did come out and say they were sick of the betting and match-fiddling that had been going on but they have never been able or willing to prove anything. I suppose eventually the whole truth will come out although it could take years. The facts will emerge one day and everyone will know that we were telling the truth. It could be 10 years after the event or 20 or 30, but we will eventually be vindicated. Hopefully I'll be well and truly retired by then.

I do not think international cricket has been harmed by the Malik affair. I did not hear any rumours about match-fixing at the World Cup in 1996. It seemed clean. Hopefully cricket around the world will stay like that. As far as I'm concerned that's it; it's over. But I would like to thank the Australian public for supporting Mark, Tim and me so well. The public has always been fantastic in their support for me and I hope I can entertain them for a few more years yet.

'TJ'

Terry Jenner is the best spin bowling coach I've met — by a country mile.
In fact during Australia's Test series against the West Indies in Australia in
1996–7 Terry, or 'TJ' as most cricket people call him, became widely known
as the 'Spin Doctor'. Ian Healy's nickname for him caught on pretty well.

TJ had watched me bowl in the First Test in Brisbane and spotted a few
problems with my action. I was coming back after a winter recuperating
from surgery on my spinning finger and my confidence in the finger and
my form was not up to scratch. When you're not confident about your body
you often make compromises with your action and that in turn affects how
the ball comes out of your hand. I bowled only reasonably well in Brisbane,
although I was happy to get through the game without any major problems with my finger. For me another hurdle in a long obstacle race had been
negotiated. But watching on television back home in Adelaide, TJ saw a
few things he did not like. He was due to come to Sydney to commentate
on ABC Radio and so he fronted at the nets. Naturally enough, as soon as
the media spotted us together the speculation began. It was fair enough, in
the sense that we were working on a few things and anyone who'd seen me
bowl before knew I was not at my best in Brisbane.

TJ said my bowling in the First Test had been fine … if I had been
making my debut.

"But because it is you," he said, "your expectations are higher and everyone else's expectations are higher. You looked like you were just putting the
ball there rather than really spinning it out of your hand. I know that's a
psychological thing about your finger. And only you know how much it
hurts. You've got to get your head right about all that before you can relax
and bowl like you used to."

The main problem was that because I was tentative in my action, either
the balls were not spinning with the zip and fizz of old and therefore dying
on the pitch or I was bowling too many loose balls. TJ knows how much
I hate bowling bad balls. I pride myself on how few bad balls I bowl.
Generally batsmen have to play a good shot to score runs off me and that's

how I like it. The less bad balls you bowl the more chance you have of building up pressure, which is how you get wickets. Any leg-spinner, any bowler really, is going to bowl the odd bad delivery. No one is perfect. Yet a good Test bowler should not bowl many. As you rise through the ranks you can judge the standard by how many bad balls are bowled per over. In first grade at club level, you get about three bad balls an over; in Sheffield Shield one an over; in Test cricket it would be more like one every two overs. The quality is generally higher because the batsmen are that much better.

In Brisbane, instead of producing a full arc in flight, dipping the ball in the air towards the leg-side before spinning it back, I was just pushing it out of my hand rather than really propelling it. Essentially it was a matter of confidence. TJ asked Heals to move to a spare net and told me to bowl at him with no run-up, just spin the ball out of my hand. All I was using was my hand. That simple exercise got me back to a few basics of my hand action and in the Sydney Test some of the old spin and dip in the air re-turned. TJ said he could see it clearly on replays.

I felt an improvement in the first innings in Sydney and in the second I thought I bowled really well. Taking the crucial wicket of Chanderpaul (one of my best ever) in the final over before lunch on the last day, after he'd hit me out of the attack half an hour earlier gave me a lot of confi-dence, especially because I gave that big leg-break everything and it spun a long way out of the rough.

About six weeks later, TJ came down to the nets in Melbourne during the one-day series, a few days after Brian Lara had hit me for three sixes in a one-dayer in Perth. The media began speculating that my confidence was down, damaged by Lara, and we'd called TJ in to help again. But he was in Melbourne that day anyway and just came down to see how I was going. No hidden agenda there. It was no big deal, nor were the three sixes by Lara. It's the nature of one-day cricket and Lara was batting well.

I received some unexpected but valuable help from TJ at lunch on the fourth day of the First Test in Johannesburg this year. After a quick bite to eat I'd gone out to the nets for a few throw downs then a short bowl. I knew I'd be bowling later that day so I wanted to stay loose. TJ, who was in South Africa working as a commentator, was doing a lap of the ground and came over to say g'day. He said he thought I'd bowled well in the first innings but had noticed that I was landing my front foot too far across to the right, pointing it at midwicket rather than fine leg. That meant I had to come over my body too far. It's a fine line but it affects your balance and direction. TJ said I had to open up that front foot a little and brace it more

In the 1993 Ashes series I had Robin Smith caught by Mark Taylor just a few balls after THAT ball, the one that got Mike Gatting ... but, I still think the Smith ball was just as good as the one that got all the attention.

RIGHT:
Getting Graham Gooch, bowled
around his legs, in 1993 was sweet,
but getting South Africa's Jacques
Kallis the same way at Jo'burg in 1997
was just as sweet - it sortof silenced
the critics who said I'd 'lost it'.

BELOW:
England's Alec Stewart, a victim
of my favourite 'flipper' at the 'Gabba
in 1994.

**Time out during
a coaching class
in South Africa,
1994.**

LEFT & BELOW:
With Fanie de Villiers,
helping out for charity
in 1994; elsewhere
on the tour it was the
in-your-face attention
of the public that
sometimes got up my
nose. This breakdown
on the veldt might
have been a sign of
things to come.

OPPOSITE:
Pressure at Jo'burg.

**What became known as The Hudson Incident. I 'lost it'.
I did the wrong thing. I'm still not sure why.**

**OPPOSITE:
Ready for anything. Pre-season training for cricket has
changed somewhat from the good old days.**

RIGHT, BELOW & OPPOSITE: The Australian team's tour to Pakistan in 1994 was a real stretch of emotions. It had everything. Playing with the cricket-mad local youngsters was a ball, and coaching them a source of great satisfaction. There was success – Akram Raza leg before, and there was disaster – 'Heals' missed a stumping, the ball went for four byes, and we lost the First Test by a sole wicket. And, of course, there was the Salim Malik bribery business.

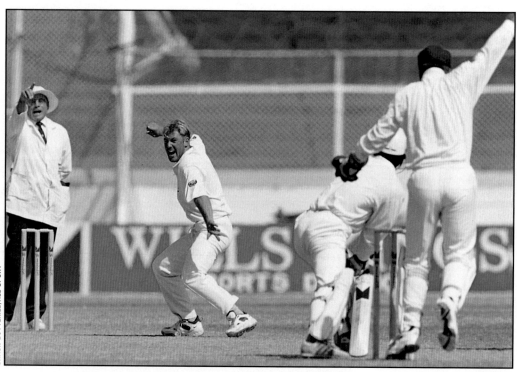

A Test hat-trick. David Boon's great catch to dismiss England's
Devon Malcolm in the 1994-95 Ashes series.

ABOVE & OPPOSITE:
Magic Moments, clockwise from above. The hat-trick ball - and,
a fistful of good cheer. Taking the catch that sent Brian Lara
on his way in the Boxing Day Test of 1996. Turning and
bouncing them at Sabina Park, Jamaica, 1995, so much so
that Ian Healy put on a helmet!

On the beach in the Caribbean, practising for
what I knew I'd be copping out in the middle of
the Test arena.

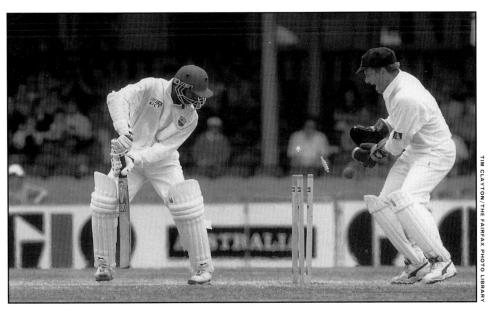

Sometimes in cricket something happens that gives you a real lift. This was one of those moments. I've bowled Shivnarine Chanderpaul last ball before lunch on the last day of the Second Test against the West Indies at the SCG in 1996. A big turner out of the rough. Suddenly the operation on my spinning finger seemed just a distant memory.

so I could bring my weight over the leg more forcefully. After I'd had a hit I asked a young boy in the crowd to go down the back of the net and fetch the ball while I bowled a few overs. It was the first time I'd had a good chat to TJ for a while and again he was able to fine-tune my action just enough to make a difference.

Generally during a season I would ring TJ once every couple of weeks to see how he thought I was going; and he would ring me if he saw something wrong. And these days he is allowed into the nets to work closely with me if we feel I need it. If a guy in the team thinks a certain person might be able to help, he can tell Swampy, who'll organise it. As well, people like Dennis Lillee, Ian Chappell or TJ are free to speak to Swampy if they see something. There are many good cricket brains and good coaches in Australia and it seems crazy to keep them away from the Australian team. Of course it has to be done properly and under the coach's eye otherwise it could get out of hand. That is how it's done now and it works very well.

For any player to feel fully comfortable with a coach, he really needs to like him and to know him well. TJ and I are very good mates, soul brothers I suppose and that goes back to our first meeting during my days at the Academy in Adelaide.

I had just returned from the Youth tour to the West Indies in 1990 and

TJ had just got out of gaol for embezzlement. He'd been sentenced to about 18 months in a low security prison while some big businessmen seem to get off very lightly for much worse offences. It was obviously a tough time for him and he felt uncomfortable about returning to the cricket world.

TJ and I met first at an Academy coaching session and we hit it off immediately. We are fairly similar people, larrikins I suppose. We like a good time, have a sense of humour, enjoy a little stirring, a few beers and a punt. The most curious thing about the similarities is that we back the same numbers at casinos. Maybe he likes me and follows my career closely because he can see both the similarities and the differences between us.

From what I understand TJ would have played more than nine Tests (for 24 wickets) if he had believed in himself more. His record for South Australia is tremendous so there is no doubt he was a fine bowler. At Test level he must have struggled to feel at ease and to gain a regular spot. A few times he had great Shield seasons but somehow missed selection for a tour when that would have given him more time settle into the team and the international game. He did take 5/90 in the Fifth Test in Port-of-Spain, Trinidad in 1972–3 and three of those were Roy Fredericks, Alvin Kallicharan and Rohan Kanhai, a very useful trio. He often says, "I took 24 Test wickets and I can remember every one. That's a worry. You don't really want to be able to remember every Test wicket you took."

In those early days in Adelaide TJ and I spent a lot of time sitting at his place talking about cricket and life in general, about our liking for a bet and for a few too many beers. A turning point in my career came one night in early 1992 — after I'd played my couple of Tests against India. We talked in depth that night at TJ's house, sitting on the couch, each with a cricket ball in hand. We showed each other various grips and delivery actions. That was when TJ noticed how fast my wrist and hand snapped when I bowled.

That night TJ said that I'd played for Australia after only playing half a dozen first-class games.

"A lot of blokes spend years in Shield cricket doing well and never get that opportunity," he said. "And there you are pissing it up against a wall, going out late at night and eating the wrong foods. Wake up to yourself and don't waste the chance you've been given."

Then when I was chosen for the tour to Sri Lanka he said, "Shit mate, I made 400 runs and took 40 wickets in a couple of Shield seasons and never got picked on the tour that followed. Some blokes only get one chance. You're very lucky because you're getting a second chance. You have got to make the most of it."

Terry Jenner, my friend the spin doctor.

TIM CLAYTON/THE FAIRFAX PHOTO LIBRARY

That advice helped me to wake up and decide to give it a red hot go and see how well I could do. My old man always said that no matter what you do, give it a go and see what you can really do. Don't have any regrets later. That is what I decided to do with cricket. Soon after I spent those months training six days a week before going on the tour to Sri Lanka later that year.

The aspect of TJ as a coach that impressed me from the start was that he could do anything he suggested to me. Sometimes when someone says to try this but cannot do it himself you tend to dismiss the idea. With TJ he would suggest — not dictate — something then show me how to do it. He never said and still never says that this is right and you must do it. He offers a suggestion and leaves it up to me. I appreciate that space and because of that we work well together. As a tip for young cricketers, the best advice I can give is to listen, then make up your mind as to whether the advice suits you. If it does, act on it. If it doesn't, say thanks and move on.

Ian Chappell says that TJ has one of the best cricket brains going around, not just on spin bowling but on the game in general. And Ian saying that means it is a major compliment. Occasionally TJ gets on his high horse and is a pain in the neck, but I let him know quickly. And we all do that now and again, don't we? When I tell him I reckon he's talking nonsense he'll be annoyed for a while before settling down again. A friendship without the occasional argument is not much of a friendship. I keep in regular contact with TJ, usually ringing him from wherever I am to see what he's thinking and whether he has spotted anything that needs attention.

One tactic TJ always emphasises is to think up, spin up. When I am not bowling well it is usually because my arm falls too low. Whenever I'm not going too well, I tell myself to think high, spin up and my arm goes higher and I spin the ball up rather than spin it down. TJ is also strong on having a plan about bowling to batsmen. My basic plan is to work batsmen across the crease. I might start with a ball on leg stump, then another, then one on middle and leg, then one on middle then maybe throw one wide of off stump. That way you find out whether he is prepared to play through the on-side against the spin. Or to another batsman I might start on off stump, then middle-and-off, then middle then throw one wide of leg stump. Normally I start with a plan for every batsman. Even if I have not played against an international batsman I'll have seen some video of him or heard a fair bit about him on the grapevine so I know where to start.

Another of TJ's tricks is designed to confuse a batsman who has not played against me before. When he is at my end I bowl a very obvious wrong'un. In that situation the batsman at my end will be watching my hand for as long as he can before switching his eyes to the action at the other end. The new man will try to see up close what I'm doing with my hands and with the ball. The main reason is that the new batsman sees the ball spin both ways, and when he hasn't seen you before he can become tentative. Then I'll give him a few top spinners that look like wrong'uns out of the hand. When they don't spin the way he expects he can become confused and start wondering just what is really going on. When he's in that state of mind he is ripe for a few special wicket-taking deliveries. I might then add to his confusion and the pressure on him by doing a little ooohing and aaahing as if he is very lucky to still be out there.

TJ now is a very good friend as well as my bowling coach. Ian Healy is pretty close to him as well. These days TJ organises a pre-Test breakfast in Adelaide which has grown from a small function to a large, popular one. Heals and I try to go each year and other players like Merv Hughes and Jonty Rhodes have been along as well. They are great mornings. And it was at a breakfast in Adelaide, a much smaller one, that TJ organised for me to meet his former Test captain, Ian Chappell, who is now also a good friend and adviser.

Mentors

Late night revellers in Cairns in northern Queensland might have seen an unusual sight one night in the spring of 1996. At about 1.30am, Ian Chappell was coaching me in slips fielding in the middle of the Cairns Mall as we walked back to our hotel after a night out. We were in the far north for the first Super 8s tournament. I had asked Ian, one of the greatest slips fielders of all time, for some advice, so there he was in the mall in the middle of the night showing me his stance and how to stay balanced in the slips. What's that old saying about you never stop learning about cricket?

Ian had always been one of my favourite cricketers. As a kid playing in the backyard with my brother Jason, 'Ian' was one of our regulars. Ian Chappell, Ian Botham, Viv Richards and Dennis Lillee were our favourites because they were players who always gave it their all. They were passionate cricketers who always had a red hot go. Part of our backyard ritual was imitating the actions and gestures of the famous players. If I were Ian Chappell, I'd have to have my shirt collar turned up and I'd scratch the turf hard when taking block, tap the wicket down, fiddle with my protector, check my collar, then chew my gum as the bowler ran in. The first shot would always be the defiant Ian Chappell hook shot.

When, during my stint at the Cricket Academy in Adelaide in 1990, Terry Jenner asked whether I'd like to meet Ian Chappell I jumped at the chance. TJ organised a breakfast with Ian at the Hilton Hotel for me and a fellow Academy player called Scott Moody. That morning Ian talked about how important it was for a cricketer to get to know himself. Know yourself: know what you need to do to prepare for a game — whether it is a few beers, an early night, a quiet meal, staying off the grog or whatever. The point was to find what suited you and your game best and do it.

I saw Ian off and on for a few years after that, mainly on the cricket circuit, but it was not until we went to the US Masters golf tournament in Augusta, Florida in 1996 that we became good friends. Ian was commentating for Channel Nine and I was there to look and learn as part of my work with Nine. We stayed together and had a few beers most nights at a little pub down the road from the house we were living in. Ian knew I didn't like Indian food, but one night he said he would take me to an Indian restaurant and order for me. He said I'd enjoy it at last. He learned something about me that night.

Despite his best efforts I didn't like the food and eventually ordered some French fries from the Indian waiter. The chips looked excellent and as I hadn't eaten much that day I scoffed them down. But they were the hot and spicy variety rather than your classic French fries and I needed something else. I told Ian I'd be back in a couple of minutes before ducking out of the restaurant and going around the corner to order a pizza. I played a few video games in that shop while waiting for the pizza and when I eventually returned to the restaurant and explained where I'd been Ian was amazed at my dietary habits. He was not the first. My love of toasted cheese sandwiches has become legendary in cricket circles and I'll often knock back an invitation to go to a restaurant with a few of the guys in the team to stay in my room and enjoy a good feed of toasted sangers.

During that stay in Augusta I told Ian that I was not happy with my batting. He agreed that I should score more runs and that I was a better batsman than my record for Australia suggested. He offered to coach me when we got back to Australia and his theory was that the West Indies had ruined my batting. I used to hook and pull but the West Indians were too quick for that and I hadn't really worked out any alternative. As he said, they've done the same to dozens of batsmen, most of them better than me. The West Indies were coming out for a five-Test series the following summer so I had to get to work on my batting. Also I had been worried that if I didn't learn to play the short ball better I might get hit on my spinning fingers and not be able to bowl. Even a slight knock on the finger that had been operated on could cause me serious problems. Ian and Rod Marsh agreed that what I had to do was work out a way of scoring off the West Indian quicks. I wanted to be able to play the hook shot as one way of countering them and, not surprisingly, Ian agreed. He said I should come over to the Academy when he was going to be there for his annual batting week. I was there for three days and spent most of the time facing short fast bowling. Not long after I went in for my first bat, Ian stopped me and we swapped over. I threw the ball at him and he showed me how to play the hook and where to put my feet. I'd been getting my feet into the wrong position, but Ian thought that the fact that I learned quickly meant I had always been able to hook properly. I'd just got into bad habits.

In one of our cricket conversations in Augusta Ian said I would not be able to bowl to him without a deep midwicket. I said I'd never used a fieldsman in that position and that no matter who was batting I would not have a fieldsman out there in Test matches. I preferred to leave that spot open to encourage batsmen to hit against my spin. He reckoned I would need one against him so we decided that when we were back in Australia we'd have a net to sort it out. So during those three days in Adelaide we had our net. Ian said it would also help him understand my bowling better and that would help his commentary. So it was research as well as competition.

Ian hadn't had a hit for a while and I had a sore finger which meant I could not rip my leg-spinner. Things were about even I suppose. TJ had always told me how highly he rated Ian as a player of spin bowling, how well he used his feet. Brad Hogg was there with us and Ian was able to get to Hoggie and cover drive him pretty well. I noticed that and decided I wouldn't give him anything on or outside off stump.

"Right, what field have you got?" Ian asked.

"Slip, short cover and the usual."

"What about deep midwicket?"

"Nope. Don't want one," I said. "If you can hit them out there good luck to you." There's nothing like challenging a proud batsman to add some spice to the contest.

As you would expect the session was very competitive. At first Ian played me well though I gave him nothing to drive through the off side. At one stage I gave him a short one, which he pulled for 4 through midwicket, but other than that I kept him quiet. I started trying a few variations but he handled them all well. His footwork was still very good. Finally, after I'd starved him of anything to hit for a while I threw one up outside off stump. He came down the pitch after it but misread the flight and missed. He swung around and neither of us could say for sure whether he would have been stumped.

Overall Ian showed then, years after retiring, what a fine batsman he must have been at his peak. I bowled him two flippers. I'm not sure whether he picked the first one, but he certainly picked the second. Overall he read me pretty well. He said he realised early on that I spin the ball too much for him to hit me through midwicket safely. I'd finally convinced him on that issue. Generally, he said he thought the best way to play me was from the other end — in other words, to try to work me for singles and rotate the strike to force me to try something different. He was quite good at pushing the ball towards gaps and I reckon he would have picked up quite a few singles. It would have been a game of patience, real cat-and-mouse stuff.

Bowling to Ian that day made me think about how I would have en-joyed bowling to him in his prime. And to players like Viv Richards, Ian Botham and Javed Miandad — great attacking batsmen who thrived on taking the challenge up to the bowler. I bowled a few times to Botham during the 1993 Ashes tour but he was nearing the end of his career. Unfortunately I never bowled to Viv or Javed. Viv was an awesome player but he would have given me a chance. Javed was a great player of spin with brilliant foot-work. As well, he was quite a talker out in the middle and he would have had plenty to say to me in between balls. Just the sort of situation I love.

As well, any bowler would love to have bowled to Sir Donald Bradman, to judge yourself against the very best. Who knows what the outcome would have been against any of those great players? You might be humiliated, but it would not matter. It would just be nice to see how you would go against such great attacking batsmen.

Ian Chappell has one of the best cricket brains going around so any time I talk to him about the game I learn something. Everything he says is simple, in the best possible way, and very positive. Many coaches tend to theorise too much, to think and say so many things that the issue under discussion becomes far too complicated and the player walks away more confused than when he went to the coach in the first place. Ian always says that it is a simple game and it is best to keep it as simple as you can. He thinks about the game they way he played — aggressively. Talking to guys who played under his captaincy and just getting to know him in recent times, I can tell how strong and adventurous he must have been. It would have been tre-mendous fun to have played under him. He was a superb tactician and also a natural leader, a players' man who supported his men all the way, which is a quality of all great captains.

Richie Benaud is the other brilliant cricket thinker I've had some dis-cussions with in recent years. Richie is a living legend so it was an awe-some experience meeting him for the first time. I'd watched him on television while I was growing up and had always enjoyed his commentary. He never says too much and whatever he does say is spot on. Also I knew a fair amount about his career. He was a great captain with lots of flair and a very intelli-gent bowler. He didn't spin the ball that much, but he had good control, a dangerous flipper and a good wrong'un. But most of all he was very shrewd, a master of the mind game — both as bowler and as captain. To a young leggie hoping to make his way in the game Richie Benaud seemed like some-one well worth meeting.

I was in England in 1991 and I asked Brendan McArdle if he could

BEN RADFORD / ALL SPORT

Two of my deliveries, the leg-spinner from around the wicket which I like to try to land in the rough of the footmarks, and the wrong'un. I'd love to have tried them out on the great batsmen like Viv Richards and Javed Miandad.

SHAUN BOTTERILL / ALL SPORT

introduce me to Richie. Brendan, a former Victorian allrounder and a legend in Melbourne club cricket and the English leagues, knows just about everybody in the world of cricket. If he doesn't he can introduce himself as if he knows them. Brendan took me up to the media area one day at The Oval. Richie was very friendly and put me at ease immediately by saying he had heard of me. He was busy with his work commitments so we didn't have time to chat much about bowling. He said that if ever I wanted to talk to him about cricket, to get in touch. The offer was open and that was all I wanted to hear. I'd made contact with him and knew I would feel more at ease next time I saw him.

In the weeks before and after my finger operation I kept in close contact with Richie. He knew the finger had been painful but he was also worried about the long-term effects of an operation. Once or twice Richie has left a message with my manager Austin Robertson, a great mate of Richie's, to tell me to look at a video of a certain game. I'll occasionally ring Richie to see how he thinks I'm going or to discuss a possible problem. He is always available, but never pushy. He never rings me, but he is always there if I ring him. He offers ideas and comments in that understated, quiet manner that makes his TV commentary so good. Even now that I know him fairly well, I still feel very pleased when I hear that Richie Benaud has praised me. There are few better compliments than that.

Knowing two legends like Ian Chappell and Richie Benaud and realising I can call on their store of knowledge and their sharp cricket minds is a huge bonus, an honour and a comfort. Those sort of links between great players of the past and the current cricketers should happen more often. The commentators enjoy a great view from up in the box and they have access to replays so they are in a good position to assess how we are playing. I can understand that none of them want to impose their views on us. All of them will offer advice but only if asked for it. That is fair enough. I wish more of the current players made close contact with past players. We are all busy and finding the time can be difficult, but there is a huge store of experience and knowledge out there that can be very helpful. Tapping into that knowledge has certainly helped me.

If a player is lucky to come into Test cricket under a great captain, that experience will stay with him forever. I was fortunate in that way and the leader in my case was Allan Border, Australia's most experienced cricketer. AB led Australia in a world record 93 Tests, more than most cricketers play, let alone captain. AB was already a legend when I first met him at a Prime Minister's game in Canberra. He was one of those great players I used to imitate in the backyard, so starting my Test career under him was a power-ful experience. The thing that stood out to me was AB's determination. He was a tough little bloke, a great fighter whose pride in playing for Australia was his greatest motivation. Just watching the way AB played inspired me. He was never a guy to stand up and shout all these words of wisdom at the team. That was not his style. Yet if you were sitting at the bar having a one-on-one chat with him, he could be very inspiring. AB is quite a shy bloke. That is why people sometimes never really got to know him well. If you found yourself alone with him or in a small group in a quiet corner some-where or if you asked him if you could have a chat with him he would feel more comfortable and start to open up. That's when you'd learn a lot from Allan Border.

I think AB has relaxed a lot more since he has retired. Now he's not under that pressure he can be one of the boys to a greater degree and that is what he has always enjoyed most about the game — not the records and the adulation, but the company of other cricketers. Most great captains influence their players' off-field lives in some way. I've heard that some of

Allan Border ... he was my first Test captain, and when I was young I used to imitate his style of play in the backyard ... a powerful influence on my career.

Ian Chappell's old teammates will ring him for advice on a business or personal matter. AB has influenced my life in several important areas away from cricket. It was on his advice that I changed my manager a few years ago to Austin Robertson — the former South Melbourne full-forward who still manages AB, Dennis Lillee, and Greg Ritchie. That was a very successful move for me and has made life much more enjoyable. I try to ring AB every few weeks to see how he is going and what he thinks about my bowling. He's a very close friend and I'll always stay in contact with him.

As my first captain AB instilled in me that playing well out there in the middle was the most important thing. Sure it's great to win endorsements and earn a good income while you're still in the spotlight, but in the end if you're achieving things on the field the rest will take care of itself. That was very much the way AB looked at international cricket and his results were beyond comparison. I worry that some players become distracted from the main game — succeeding on the field — by the lure of promotional work and earning extra money. We all need to earn money to survive but when the extra work starts to detract from the bread and butter stuff of actually playing cricket well, your career will soon be in trouble.

As a teammate one thing which always impressed me about AB was his attitude to practice. He always played as well as possible in the nets and I thoroughly enjoyed bowling to him. Apart from a couple of close decisions that we agree to disagree on, I only dismissed him once in the nets. It was always a challenge to keep him quiet during a practice session. He was always working at getting on top of a bowler and if you were bowling well he'd work at pushing singles much as he would in a game. It was always a contest with AB, even in the nets, and after a session you felt like you'd had a decent workout, that you'd stretched yourself in some way. And that is the way you improve.

The other area where AB helped my game was that his comments on my bowling were made from a batsman's point of view. It is one thing for a former bowler like Terry Jenner to watch my bowling closely and spot technical things, but quite another for a batsman to assess me. AB was tremendous at that, suggesting things I could try that would confuse or upset batsmen or tactics which would counter the way a batsman would be thinking. Bowling at Test level is very much a cat-and-mouse game where the smallest advantages can make a difference. Learning from AB how a batsman might think about playing me gave me those sort of advantages and often kept me half a step ahead of the game.

Apart from Merv Hughes, a long time friend from Melbourne, my two best mates in cricket these days are the Waugh brothers, Mark and Steve. Mark is very similar to me, laid back, likes a punt, enjoys spending his time doing the same things I enjoy. We often go out together, usually for a feed then to the races or a casino. On days off we'll often grab a fourth player and have a hit of tennis or maybe play a round of golf. It is always pretty competitive, especially the tennis, as the Waughs played for New South Wales at school level before cricket took over as their main career.

In the ratings which came out after Australia's series win in South Africa, Steve and Mark were number 1 and 2, the best two batsmen in the world. I don't always treat those ratings systems too seriously but I reckon they have it right on this point.

On his day Mark is probably the best batsman in the world. I still rate the hundred he made for New South Wales against Victoria on a spinning pitch in Sydney a few years ago as one of the best innings I've seen. I spun the ball a long way that day and did not give Mark much to hit, but he kept his patience in frustrating conditions and made a very fine century. His two other great innings are his hundred in Jamaica in the Fourth Test in 1995 which helped give us that famous series victory over the West Indies. Steve made a great, courageous 200 at the other end to give the innings its foundation while Mark rarely made a mistake in scoring his runs quickly. They dominated the West Indian fast bowlers and set us up for a great win. Equally as important was Mark's century at Port Elizabeth in 1997, a long, controlled and confident innings on a pitch every other batsman in the game found very difficult. In those situations Mark rises to the challenge and his sheer class — in technique, reflexes and shot-making — come to the fore. In my opinion that's his best innings.

Steve has developed into a different style of batsman to Mark. Their partnership in Jamaica is the best example of that. While Mark took a few risks and took the game away from the bowlers, Steve was the rock, minimising his risks and forcing the bowlers to bowl to him. It's the perfect combination for a big partnership and their teammates want nothing more than to sit back and watch both the Waughs make runs together.

I find Stephen Waugh a very funny bloke. People say he never smiles on the field and never seems to enjoy himself much but that is just how he appears. He's not like that at all. He's a tough competitor, no doubt about that. But he's also a very witty character who breaks me up with some of his one-liners. He has a sharp mind and his comments usually go straight to the heart of the matter. Both the Waughs have a dry sense of humour, but although you might expect that from someone as laidback as Mark,

RAY TITUS/NEWS LTD

The Waugh twins, Steve and Mark after their great 231-run partnership in the Jamaica Test match, 1995.

you don't necessarily expect it from someone as determined and focused as Steve. I think Steve will be an excellent vice-captain, and I wish him all the best, because he is a close friend.

Steve has been Australia's best batsman for the past three or four years. Magnificent and very consistent in all conditions. The batting tends to revolve around him as the senior man now that David Boon has followed Allan Border into retirement. Like both those great players, Steve has had his tough times, lost form and been dropped. But his fighting instincts run deep and he has fought his way back brilliantly. In those past few years he has averaged something like 60 in Test cricket — absolutely outstanding. When he walks out to bat for Australia the rest of us know how determined and proud he is. Like AB before him, Steve is an inspiration to his teammates. A great cricketer.

Steve has taken it on himself to be Glenn McGrath's personal batting coach and I suppose I'm second on his list. He has tried to help me improve and at times I must have sent him crazy with frustration. I often field between the Waughs in the slips — Mark at second, me at third and Steve in the gully. I'll often talk to Steve about selections, where the team is going, even about the politics that surround the team. We might not agree with some of the things being done but we also realise that often there is not much the players can do about some aspects of the scene.

I certainly think the players need to be consulted more on tour programming and the amount of cricket we are playing in such a short space of time. Hopefully the Australian Cricket Board and the new Players' Association can work together. Fingers crossed.

Mates

From the time I first played competition cricket at school I've always enjoyed the company of other cricketers. It's an important part of the game, the part that stays with you after you've finished playing. You only have to recall what it's like when former teammates and opponents get together at a function to appreciate how much they enjoy each other's company. I love watching older players exaggerate about how good they were back in the old days before leg-spinners and fast bowlers wore earrings.

It is no surprise that teammates enjoy seeing each other, but I suppose some people might be surprised at how well former opponents get on with each other once their playing days are over. Yet it shouldn't be a surprise. One of cricket's best attributes is that it brings people together — from different country towns, from different suburbs of a city, from different states of a country and from different parts of the world. It's the same process no matter the level and it's a part of the game I still enjoy. Playing international cricket gives you the chance to travel to parts of the world and encounter lifestyles you'd never see otherwise. And it gives you the chance to make friends with people you would never have met had it not been for cricket.

Of all the friends from other countries I've made while playing for Australia, the closest would be South Africa's Jonty Rhodes. At some stage during the Test series in Australia in 1993–4 I ended up in a dressingroom after a day's play next to Jonty and we hit it off immediately. They say opposites attract and in this case it seems to be true. Jonty is completely different to me. We're both happy, fun-loving people who can find something to laugh about in most situations, but that's about it for similarities. Jonty is very religious and I'm not. He doesn't drink much or gamble whereas I dabble a little there to let off steam occasionally. He's a batsman and I'm not — well, not a specialist anyway.

Perhaps it was the way Jonty played his cricket on that tour, especially the way he fielded with all that energy and flair, that made me think this bloke was worth getting to know. Like most of the South Africans, Jonty loves to sweep and it didn't take long for him to mention that out in the middle when I was bowling to him.

"Right Warnie, the sweepathon's on," he would say.

"Okay Jonty, you're on."

Other times he'd speak Afrikaans during play just to annoy us. All I could say in retaliation was, "Jonty, if you're gonna sledge me, at least sledge me in English."

Maybe I should've tried replying to him in Australian rhyming slang.

When Jonty was in India in late 1996 playing in the one-day series against Australia and the host nation, he rang me in Melbourne about half a dozen times to see how I was doing after my finger operation. On the 1997 tour I had dinner with him and his wife at his place in Durban during our game against Natal. He was in good form on and off the field. He was hitting the ball well and forced his way back into the team for the First Test. But the selectors only gave him that one chance and we didn't play against him until the one-day series later in the tour. I'm sure Jonty will return to Australia for South Africa's tour in the 1997–8 summer. They need him.

Darren Gough is another player I've become good friends with, although I haven't seen him for a while. I liked the look of Goughie in the First Test in Brisbane in 1994–5. He showed some courage and enthusiasm and I respected him for that. He is a bright personality on and off the field and a real goer on it. England needs more like him.

I had heard that Goughie was a big hitter and after he'd blocked an over or two against me in that First Test in Brisbane I told him I'd heard a lot about his power-hitting. He didn't say anything back and he didn't try to belt me out of the park, but when he hooked Craig McDermott for 6 in the Sydney Test he turned towards me and smiled. He couldn't resist it and fair enough too. He was Man of the Match in that dramatic game and by that stage he'd won over the Australian public with his enthusiasm. Soon after he broke his foot running in to bowl in a one-day game in Melbourne and had to go home. The day before the Fourth Test in Adelaide which England needed to win to stay in the series, Goughie sent me a fax from wintry Yorkshire to wish me luck, to say it had been a pleasure to play against me and to tell me that England were going to win the match. They did too, thanks to a fine all-round performance by Phil DeFreitas and some very fast bowling by Devon Malcolm. Goughie struggled for a couple of years after that foot injury, but returned to the England team early in 1997 and immediately added strength and character to the side. Hopefully we'll be playing against each other for a few years yet.

Brian McMillan is another very good bloke who doubles as one of the best cricketers in the world. 'Big Mac' is one of the toughest competitors around. He loves a stoush out on the field and is not shy about telling opponents what he thinks of them. But he always sledges with style and humour.

In the Third Test in Adelaide in 1994 he and I had some fun during a game Australia had to win to save the series. At one stage Brian refused to take a third run off a sweep by Peter Kirsten, which meant he stayed with me at the bowler's end.

"Eh mate, you can run three. Don't be scared," I said.

When he refused a single soon after that I asked him if he was too scared to get down the other end and face me.

"Listen Warnie, people disappear every day in South Africa. One more won't make any difference," he said. "I'm going to take you fishing over there. You're going to be the bait." I don't think I said much after that.

Brian was the one who borrowed a security guard's rifle and came to the door of our dressingroom one lunch break in the Johannesburg Test in 1994 and said he was sick of us.

"Right, that's it. I've had you blokes."

More than a few heads ducked for cover at the sight of such a big mean-looking McMillan armed to the teeth.

The Australian team respects Brian for his ability, his competitive instincts and his sense of humour. He never takes a backward step in the tightest situations and that is why he is such a good player, probably the best all-rounder in the world.

During the 1995 tour of the West Indies, Brian Lara and I spent some time together and formed a friendship. Brian took me around to a few places, giving me another inside look at life in the Caribbean. I suppose he and I have something in common in that we tend to attract publicity. He has found it hard to handle at times, especially when you add the huge expectations on him every time he goes out to bat.

During his disappointing tour of Australia two years later, we played a few rounds of golf together but things got a bit heated in the Fifth Test in Perth when Brian complained publicly about Australia's sledging. As if some of the West Indians haven't sledged Australians over the years.

As I said at the time, Brian lost a few points with me over that one. It would have been far better if he'd come to see us after play and said his piece. To do so to the media forced us to defend ourselves, as captain Mark Taylor did at his post-match press conference. This coming on top of the incident in Sydney when he stormed across to our dressingroom and told our team manager Ian McDonald and coach Geoff Marsh to tell Ian Healy he was no longer welcome in their rooms was way over the top. Heals caught him fair and square and Brian was given out by the umpires. Basically he accused Heals of cheating and the fact that he never apologised greatly upset all the Australian players. The West Indies manager Clive Lloyd didn't know what Brian Lara had done. Once he found out he was furious. He nailed Brian, and apologised to McDonald and Marsh. But Brian still didn't apologise. If you make a mistake, no matter who you are, you must be man enough to admit it.

Many people do not agree with the view that what happens on the field should stay there. Admittedly television shows the viewer a lot of what goes

Body language. In the heat of a moment in the middle at the WACA relations between Brian Lara and me became a little less friendly than they'd been before.

on between opponents in the heat of the moment, although it never shows all of it. Despite all that, Brian and I are still mates. I was criticised for giving Daryll Cullinan a couple of send-offs in 1993–4, but the cameras never showed that he started it. If someone wants to try to put me off my game then I will not lie down and accept it. If they choose to live by the sword they have to be prepared to die by it. They cannot complain about that. The same applies to me.

As for Brian, I'm sure that he will realise that he could have handled things better on the tour to Australia. He was certainly under enormous pressure to make runs and he only managed to do that in the second innings in the Fourth Test and in the Fifth, but by then it was too late. Australia had taken the series. Maybe Glenn McGrath can have a bit of a spell over Brian like I have over Darryl Cullinan.

When you carry such expectations on your back, a run of poor form can be very hard to handle, but it is part of life at this level and usually in the long run makes you a better person and a better player.

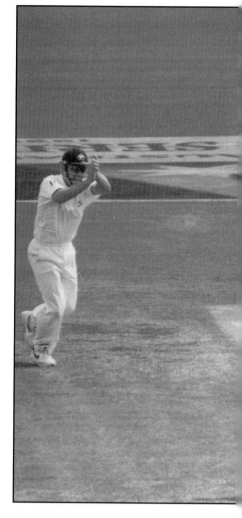

Brian is a brilliant player and I always enjoy the challenge of playing against him. As well, it would be a shame for our friendship to end simply because of one incident in a tough Test match.

Because we do not play Pakistan, India and Zimbabwe as often as South Africa, England and West Indies, my friendships with fellow leg-spinners Mushtaq Ahmed, Anil Kumble and Paul Strang have not had time to develop. But we do share the common bond of being leg-spin bowlers and whenever we can we spend time together swapping ideas about bowling and generally giving each other encouragement. More of that later.

STEVE CHRISTO/THE FAIRFAX PHOTO LIBRARY

ABOVE: Brian Lara, caught Healy bowled Warne, the Adelaide Test, 1997. He made 78. That score, and one in the Perth Test, failed to save what was a difficult tour for him.

RIGHT: When the going gets tough team-mates stick together. Paul Reiffel and I share the bitterness of a loss at Trinidad in 1995.

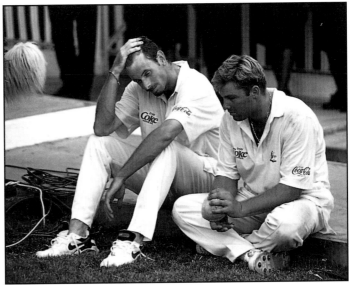

SHAUN BOTTERILL/ALL SPORT

Mind Games

Someone pointed out to me a couple of years ago that in an article Greg Chappell said he thought I had the same attitude to bowling as Dennis Lillee, that fierce competitive feeling Dennis had towards batsmen, the way he built himself to a pitch of concentration and emotion when he bowled. I took Greg's comment as a major compliment. Anyone would. That sort of "hate" towards batsmen is always associated with fast bowlers and most people assume spinners are quieter, more thoughtful types. Perhaps that is why some people think I'm arrogant and overly aggressive out in the middle. Well, I'm a bowler first and foremost.

In some ways fast bowlers will always be ferocious competitors. When you're running in 30 metres about 120 times on a hot day with your knees, back and feet aching and you're trying to extract life from a flat, concrete-hard pitch, you're not going to think twice about hurting the feelings of the poor batsman at the other end. Fast bowling is the most physical part of cricket and the quicks work very hard. I think they're entitled to be mean.

Most spinners only bowl off a few steps and I would have one of the shortest run-ups of any spinner. So why get so worked up?

Well, mainly because it is still a contest between bat and ball whether a quick or a slow bowler is operating. Bill O'Reilly, the great Australian leg-spinner of the 1930s, used to appeal like a fast bowler. Bill was a big man who bowled fast leggies off a fairly long run-up. People who saw him said he did not appeal to an umpire, he demanded the decision. And any batsman who hit even a single off him was liable to cop a few well chosen words. Good spinners need to be passionate about what they do even if some prefer to keep that passion under a lid most of the time.

All cricketers enjoy one-day games. They're exciting, lively, popular and good fun. But every cricketer will also tell you that the ultimate test of your ability comes in Test matches. Tests go for five days and there is no place to hide. Things happen quickly in one-day games and there is little or no time

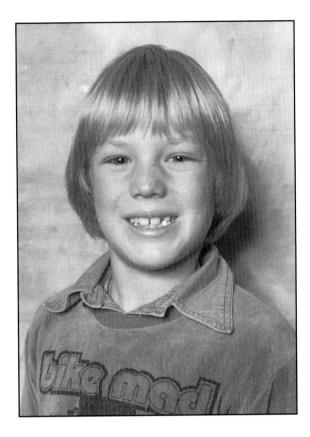

At primary school ... maybe there was a little bit of determination even then.

for a bowler to work on a batsman, to play a few tricks on him, con him or induce a false sense of security. If I believe I have the edge over a batsman and that he has a fatal flaw, I know that in a Test match I will have time to work on that flaw, expose it and dismiss the batsman. In a one-day game I might not have that time nor the freedom to work on the batsmen because you're also trying to protect boundaries. The priority in one-day games is to restrict runs, and although taking wickets is probably the best way to do that, you have to find a balance between attacking for wickets and keeping the runs to a minimum.

In Test matches there is no better aspect than the one-on-one contest between a bowler and a batsman. Cricket is a team game but within that there are all sorts of one-on-one, personal contests. They add enormously to the drama, not only for the public but also for the players involved. South Africa's Daryll Cullinan and I have had such a contest, as did Glenn McGrath and Brian Lara in the West Indies in 1995 and in Australia in 1996–7. The battle over several series between Steve Waugh and Curtly Ambrose has been one of the highlights of world cricket in my time — two great, mentally tough players taking each other on. Like Dennis Lillee, I thrive on that personal battle. I'm in the team to dismiss batsmen and you do that not only by bowling them good deliveries, but by working on their confidence, trying to convince them that you're better than they are and that it is only a matter of time before you dismiss them. A large part of the contest is mental and I enjoy those mind games as much as other more obvious aspects of cricket.

Mind games can vary from full-on stares and words between bowler and batsman, to tactical ploys, true or fake, to small gestures which can all build pressure. I've already mentioned Terry Jenner's idea of showing an obvious wrong'un to the batsman at my end to make him see it turn. The batsman then knows I can spin them both ways, so he tries to pick them when he gets down to face. TJ also suggested to me that it is a good idea to often start a spell without bat-pad fieldsmen. A few years ago it was the fashion for every spinner to start with at least one bat-pad in place. It looked aggressive, but often it backfired because it put more pressure on the bowler than the batsman. Unless the bowler found his accuracy from the first over, he could be hit for boundaries, because there would be gaps in the field. If that happened he had to work his way back into the contest and against good players that can be very difficult. If the bowler was forced to move his close fielders back into the ring, he was conceding a victory to the batsman.

TJ's idea is to hold back the close-in field until you are landing the ball well and your confidence has grown. With most fielders back you can dry up the singles and bowl a few maidens, by which time the pressure on the batsman has increased significantly. I always try to bowl a few big spinning leg-breaks early on to assert my authority and make the batsman worry. Once you're on the spot and bowling well then, with a dose of drama thrown in, you can move the fielders in close. The drama can come from chatting to your captain before the over but suggesting he wait until the second or third ball before you call to him — so the batsman can hear — "What do you think Tubs, bat pad?" When the captain then brings some fielders in close, the batsman knows the contest is moving to an even tougher stage.

Equally, if I have a batsman struggling and then beat him with a big leg-break that spins a long way past him, I'll make sure I let him know about it, especially on a turning pitch where I can really intimidate him. I'll throw the arms in the air, hang my head in disappointment, smirk at him knowingly or even say to my wicketkeeper, "Geez Heals, it's doing a bit today. The batsman wouldn't want to make a mistake."

On the other hand if nothing much is happening I might try to break the batsman's concentration by saying something like, "Heals, it's 150 to the green. What club?"

VIV JENKINS/AUSTRALIAN CRICKET BOARD

**Mind games ... it might be a stare, it might be
a word, or simply a small gesture.**

It's all part of the mind games that go on between deliveries and which, to me, make the game so interesting. In fact the time between deliveries can be as important as the actual deliveries.

I like to take my time during an over. I don't like to rush but then I don't like being delayed either. It's all about bowling at my rhythm, putting my pattern on the play. Often I like to get into position to start my approach then make the batsman wait for a second or so. I'll hold the ball in my hands in front of me, spin it up out of my hand once or twice, put my head down as if I'm planning something then I'll look up at the batsman and start to move in. It's a way of convincing the batsman that I'm the boss, that I'm in control of the situation. As well, that pause can make the batsman think I've got something up my sleeve, that the next ball is going to be a ripper. That's when I might grunt as I deliver the next ball to make him think I'm bowling a big leg-break when in fact it will be a top spinner. It is all about being one or two steps ahead, keeping the batsman guessing in the same way the magician David Copperfield keeps his audience guessing. Part of the art of bowling spin is to make the batsman think something special is happening when it isn't.

Another reason why the time between balls can be important is that the bowler can vary that time to suit his feelings at that particular time and also let the batsman's mind wander. If I'm in good form, confident and really bowling well, I tend to rush through my overs. I can't wait to get at the batsman so I want the next ball to come quickly. It's mainly an emotional thing, but it can also be tactically smart. If I'm on top and going well, the less time the batsman has to gather his thoughts or think about what's happening the better. I can be all over him like a rash and he won't have the time to scratch himself. In the series in the Caribbean in 1995, some of the West Indies batsmen started trying to slow me down. It annoyed me because it interrupted my rhythm. Shivnarine Chanderpaul has a habit of fiddling with his pads all the time. I don't know whether it's one of those subconscious habits most batsmen have or whether he can't get pads to fit properly or whether he simply uses it as a way of giving himself more time to prepare for the next ball. And that's good batting.

Then in the Second Test in Sydney in 1996–7, a few of the West Indian players started to fiddle around between balls. It seemed obvious to me that they were trying to slow me down and put me off my rhythm. In that situation I have to work really hard not to let it frustrate me. Instead I try to make it work for me. One thing I did a few times in Sydney was to wait until they were finally set, and then make them wait for me. It was tit for tat I suppose. You make me wait and I'll make you wait even longer.

Just as a bowler in form usually wants to get through his overs fairly quickly, a bowler who is struggling should take his time, or if the batting side is belting the bowling, the bowler should try to upset their rhythm. Yet often when you are struggling you tend to rush between balls. Michael Bevan in the Adelaide Test against the West Indies in Adelaide in 1996–7 was a case in point. It was Michael's first Test as the "official" second spinner rather than as a number six batsman and part-time bowler. His bowling was still developing — still is — and when Mark Taylor brought him on at first change in the first innings, Michael felt the pressure. He bowled some loose balls and was hit for a few boundaries. The situation seemed to be slipping away from him and I noticed that he was rushing through his overs. I had a word to him after one over and suggested he slow down a little to give himself time to think about his next delivery and to concentrate on doing the basics like getting his action right and releasing the ball properly from his hand so he can give it a rip. With two spinners in our attack we were going to get through the 90 overs pretty comfortably so there was no reason for Michael to rush. He needed time to settle and he also needed to stop bowling to the batsman's rhythm. When a batsman is on top he enjoys receiving the next ball fairly promptly. He is in a rhythm and wants the game to continue at that pace. That's when an experienced bowler will slow things down, have a chat with the captain in the middle of an over or change a few field placings partly to slow the game and partly to give the batsman something else to think about while he's waiting impatiently for the next ball.

Although some theatrics can help a bowler, they do not always work. In some situations the mind games revolve around more technical aspects. Often it's matter of knowing the batsman's technique and temperament. If a batsman loves to cut I'll often bowl my first over or two on leg-stump to starve him of his favourite shot. Then once I feel I have him under pressure and he's itching to do something, I'll give him a shorter ball just outside off-stump if he's a right-hander. But it won't be a long hop. It's usually a faster, flatter leggie. If it doesn't land properly and I get hit for 4 I can make that work for me because that boundary means that the next time he sees a short one he'll be on the backfoot and looking for another 4. He'll be set up for a quicker one or the flipper. Depending on the batsman and the situation I can react two ways to being hit for 4. I might have a go at myself for bowling a bad ball and even though I know I'm setting the guy up for a flipper you still don't like getting hit for four. The batsman thinks I've made a mistake and might make another one. Or I might just give him a knowing look which makes him think I meant to give him a short one because I am planning something. That will make him sweat on the flipper in which case I might bowl full leg-breaks and toppies for the next few overs to keep him wondering when it's coming.

Similarly you can often bowl to a batsman's strength — or the area he thinks is a strength. Graham Gooch was a good sweeper, but he also was very good at hitting me over the infield straight down the ground. A few times on turning pitches I bowled outside his leg stump tempting him to sweep even though the spin made it dangerous as he had to hit against the direction of the ball coming back in to him. I had a fieldsman in the deep to stop boundaries and another closer to stop singles and catch a top-edged sweep.

"Come on Goochie," the situation was saying to Graham, "You can't pad me away all day. You've got to sweep, but it's dangerous isn't it?"

If Goochie was worried about sweeping, he had to resist a favourite shot and pad me away. If the pitch was spinning a fair way, I was a chance to get one to turn from well outside leg stump and go behind his legs. That sort of situation becomes a game of patience. I'd give him nothing to drive and nothing on the off-side for quite a while. It was a war of nerves and on two memorable occasions I won out — once in England in 1993 when I finally bowled him behind his legs when he failed to pad up carefully enough and the other in Brisbane in 1994–5 when his frustration forced him to try to hit me over midwicket instead of sweeping — but still against the spin — and he bottom-edged it and was brilliantly caught by Ian Healy. They were two very satisfying wickets, as I rate Gooch one of the best players of leg-spin I've come across. And a great bloke as well. I always enjoyed the challenge of bowling to him and then the beer with him afterwards.

A day when I used a combination of particular conditions and knowledge of my opponents to work out a game plan was on the third day of the First Test against Pakistan in Brisbane in 1995–6. The pitch was true and bouncy but not offering much spin. Normally I prefer bowling with the wind, but on that day it was fairly stiff and the pace bowlers needed to come down. I had to bowl into the wind. Once I saw that I was not going to turn the ball far, I tried a few top-spinners. The toppies dipped quite a lot because of the wind so I decided to bowl more toppies than usual. The other reasons were that the Pakistanis like to attack spinners and most love to drive towards mid-off and mid-on. But occasionally they can be lazy with their footwork, probably because in Pakistan the pitches are slow and batsmen can adjust later than they can in Australia. I thought that if I could drop a few top-spinners on them they might not quite get to the pitch of the ball and, unable to pull out of their drives, might be caught in front of the wicket. As well, I thought the extra bounce — from the Gabba pitch and the top-spinners — might worry them when they were defending. The close-in fieldsmen in front of the pitch might then come into play.

So there it was and for once a plan worked perfectly. The toppies came out well and the wind and the pitch combined beautifully. Once the first few batsmen fell to me the rest seemed to crumble without giving themselves time to work out what I was doing and how they should play. Pakistan are prone to collapses and I was in the right place at the right time and, importantly, in the right conditions.

More than most sports these days, cricket offers tremendously varying conditions, especially in Australia — from one of the bounciest, fastest pitches in the world, the WACA at Perth, to a slow turner at the Sydney Cricket Ground, to the Melbourne Cricket Ground's seam and bounce, to the consistent and even pitches in Brisbane and Adelaide. Normally in England you either have very flat, true batting pitches or greener tracks which offer pace bowlers sideways movement. Then you have a fast, bouncy and true

EVAN COLLIS/AUSTRALIAN PICTURE LIBRARY

Fiddling with flight on the fast and bouncy WACA pitch.
Australia versus Zimbabwe in the World Series, 1994.

pitch at The Oval. New Zealand pitches are similar to English seamers and on the subcontinent the pitches are slower with less bounce, but can either spin or seam depending on the amount of preparation. Although bounce helps spinners as much as sideways spin, you must deceive the batsman in the air, especially on slow pitches.

I enjoy bowling in Perth although I've not taken as many wickets there per game as at other grounds. Certainly Perth can be a great place to bat against spin if you can handle the extra bounce. The ball always comes on to the bat so if a batsman hits through the line properly he should time the shot well. And the outfield is so fast that if he beats the infield he almost always gets 4. On a pitch like that the margin for error for a spinner is small, because if you are off-line good batsmen can use the pace of the pitch to put you away, often cutting, glancing and sweeping. It's a different challenge to those you encounter at other grounds.

The beauty of the game is the variety and the challenges that that variety presents. When you start touring the world as an international cricketer you have to learn to adjust to all those conditions and it's a part of the game that keeps you interested and working hard. If you meet those challenges you are definitely a better player. For me the most satisfying thing about that Test match against Pakistan in Brisbane was that I altered my bowling style to suit particular conditions and the tactic was successful. Every time you manage something like that you know you've taken another step along the way to becoming the best cricketer you can.

The Needle

Without doubt the most difficult cricketer I've met or played against is Sri Lanka's captain, Arjuna Ranatunga. That should come as no surprise to anyone who follows international cricket. Why? Well, the reasons go to the heart of why the Australian team thinks it is hard done by when we are roundly criticised for sledging, verbal confrontation if you like, while the dubious actions of other teams are excused or ignored.

Sledging, or chirping as the South Africans call it, is one part of the wider aspect of cricket called gamesmanship and has been in the game forever, although some people think it has no place there. I've just discussed the games I sometimes play when I'm bowling, trying to trick batsmen into thinking I'm going to do one thing when I'm planning another, or planning nothing at all. Is that fair? It's worth remembering that when the wrong'un was invented many people — no doubt batsmen — thought it was deceitful and unfair, against the spirit of the game. Well, that's how I view Ranatunga's actions — against the spirit of international cricket.

The main reason I dislike Ranatunga is that he continually interrupts play to ask for new gloves, a drink, a jumper, a new bat, another new pair of gloves and so on. Then he pleads an injury and asks for a runner. He carries too much weight and should accept the consequences. What can the umpires do? If he says he has sustained a pulled muscle during this innings how can the umpires test it? If they refused him the runner all hell would break loose. Often when he is allowed a runner, Ranatunga will smirk at us to rub it in. He knows we think he has conned the umpires and gotten away with it again. For quite a while the public in Australia seemed to ignore what he was up to. People felt sorry for the Sri Lankans, the new kids on the block, up against the tough, no-holds-barred Australians. However I think the tide has turned and people are realising that Ranatunga plays a cunning sort of game.

Arjuna Ranatunga wins the World Cup Final for Sri Lanka.
Sadly, his overt gamesmanship detracts from his achievements.

ABOVE: In 1993, I celebrated The Ashes win with 'AB' and Merv.

RIGHT: Mates. Jonty Rhodes and I hit it off in 1993-94, and it's a lasting friendship.

OPPOSITE: My friendship with Brian Lara cooled a little during the 1996-97 series when he started talking up things that had happened on the field, thus breaking the historical players' code, what happens on the field stays on the field.

PREVIOUS PAGE: Getting stuck in the World Series – but the ultimate test of a cricketer's ability is the Test match.

BEN RADFORD/ALL SPORT

ROSS KINNEARD/ALL SPORT

ABOVE & OPPOSITE:
In cricket, a game of great uncertainty, a sense of humour
can be a wonderful ally. Here's why (clockwise from above) —
I'm stumped by Kaluwitherana in the World Cup final, I've
been hit for six by Devon Malcolm in the SCG Ashes Test,
1995 and, there might be no tougher assignment in the game
than trying to beat the West Indies on their home patch.

CLIVE MASON/ALL SPORT: OPPOSITE PAGE

PREVIOUS PAGES:
Down and out in Lahore. Sri Lanka have won the
1996 World Cup final.

TRENT PARKE/NEWS LTD: PREVIOUS PAGES

**All smiles. I'd got lucky with a bowling plan against
Zimbabwe in the World Series, 1994-95.**

PREVIOUS PAGE,
THIS PAGE & OPPOSITE:
On the 1993 Ashes
tour I was offered
£25,000 just to pose
in the nets wearing
only shorts — I guess
they could have turned
up to a Mercantile
Mutual Cup match
in Australia and got
the shot for nothing!
The fashion shots
were taken by the
London *Sun* news-
paper-check out the
pebbles on the beach!
No doubt about it, the
Aussie surf has some-
thing going for it.

The Brotherhood of Legspin. With Anil Kumble and Mushtaq Ahmed at the 1996 World Cup.

ABOVE & OPPOSITE:
Cap'n Warne. Being in charge of Lloyd Williams' Crown XI –
you'll surely recognise some of the faces–was a hoot; leading
Victoria to a win in the Sheffield Shield was a celebration;
if I ever climb to the pinnacle – offered the opportunity to lead
Australia – it will be an honour.

The **MCG**, home. When my international career is over
I'd like to play a few seasons with Victoria.

Ranatunga has enormous clout in Sri Lanka. He comes from a family of politicians and has said he might end up in that field one day. He certainly has some attributes of a certain type of politician, but not one I'd waste my vote on. Most of the Sri Lankans are good blokes and 'The Guru', Asanka Gurusinha, is a real favourite with the Australian team. But Ranatunga is captain and gets what he wants. Unfortunately his attitude affects the rest of his team. The classic example of that came during that fiery World Series final in Sydney in 1995–6.

Chasing a big score after a storm, Sri Lanka were trying to thrash the bowling when Ranatunga pulled his usual trick and called for a runner. That started the trouble. Australia won that match fair and square to take the one-day finals series in two straight games — and that in the middle of a Test series Australia won 3–0, taking each Test by huge margins. Then Ranatunga showed his true colours on the field after the match when he, his coach Duleep Mendis, and Aravinda de Silva refused to shake our hands after the match. Our captain Mark Taylor walked across to where the Sri Lankans were gathered for the presentation ceremony and Tubby was furious when his offer of handshakes all round was sullenly refused. Ian Healy and I were following Tubby, but after the refusal he turned to us and said, "Don't bother."

All through my career I've been taught to play hard to win but always to accept defeat. When I've played in a losing team I've always congratulated the opposition, shaken hands and had a drink and a chat afterwards. To me the Sri Lankans' performance that night in Sydney was very, very ordinary. All summer they had whipped up sympathy about the calling for throwing of off-spinner Mutthiah Muralitharan. The Australian players seemed to cop a lot of the flak for that even though umpires around the world had been expressing concern about Murali's action privately for some years and even though the umpire who called him, Darrell Hair, had informed the International Cricket Council about his concerns a few months before the Sri Lankans' tour here. That had nothing to do with the Australian team, yet we still received lots of criticism, especially from Sri Lankan supporters. The tourists never accepted the umpire's decision (and not just in the heat of the moment, but for weeks afterwards), fed the press and so the public with every story they could to support their case and always tried to put pressure on the authorities. From what I understand, the Sri Lankans never worried about the widespread concerns about Murali's action. They wanted to call the authorities' bluff and that was that.

Muralitharan aside, what is worse for the game, what is more outside the spirit of the game? Wasting time and so denying the public the action it pays to see and constantly calling for a runner, or having some angry words to say in the heat of battle? Also the Sri Lankans have plenty to say to us when they're in the field although they usually speak in their language to annoy us even more and to avoid getting into trouble with the umpires. Then when we return the favour, they complain to the umpires that we're using "dirty words". We have never complained about the Sri Lankans or anyone else sledging us, but quite a few of them complain about us. The problem with the way we Australians do it is that we're more open about it. We don't do it on the sly, like some teams do. We're competitive and passionate and we make no apologies for that. I'm not saying we do it all the time — just when we might need to.

The worst thing is when I have a go or say something and then the batter hits me for a 4 or 6. How bad's that?

The South Africans take a similar approach to us. They're aggressive cricketers and they say a few words out in the middle. They know that we will not whinge about it and we'll give as good as we get then have a beer and a laugh about it afterwards. I've been criticised for this business of having a beer with someone after a day of exchanging angry words with the same bloke. The point is that those words are not personal. Firstly they're part of the gamesmanship that goes on, where you try to test the mettle of your opponent. Secondly they are just as much about firing ourselves up for the contest as they are about intimidating the opposition. Sledging has been going on for years and years. The players just don't take it that seriously. Not the South Africans anyway, because they understand what it is all about and they are honest about it.

One South African has come out in public to express his views about Australian sledging. Former captain Kepler Wessels played Test cricket for Australia before returning to his native South Africa. Kepler saw Australians from the inside then from the outside. In February 1997, in the early weeks of our tour to South Africa, Kepler told the press, "The Australians are very clever about their sledging. They use it not as a loss of control tool. They use it to get an advantage and they pick on people who they think will respond or will be adversely affected by it. If they think it will make you more determined or will not affect you, they won't do it."

What makes them great is that they chirp away on the field and then go away and enjoy a beer. What I had to do with them was just good wholehearted fun and tough competition — and that is how it should be. They are pretty funny. They have got a very good sense of humour. I believe sledging is a great part of cricket so long as it doesn't become too personal."

Another former Test captain has expressed similar views. At the same time as Kepler made his comments, New Zealand's Ken Rutherford said, "It worries me international match referees are trying to sanitise the game. There is a lot of character being milked from it. Ultimately I think people want to see some spice. The Australian side sledge and they use gamesmanship to their advantage but I don't believe they go over the top. I always enjoyed playing them. It was just tremendously exciting. The hard way they played brought Test cricket to fever pitch."

I think it is worth looking at a couple of incidents I've been involved in to see what lies behind them. Apart from the incident with Andrew Hudson, for which I take full responsibility, I've had run-ins with two South Africans.

We first came across Darryll Cullinan in the First Test in Melbourne in 1993–4. He'd made a triple century in South African cricket and looked like he could be their best player. Fielding in the slips in our first and only innings of that rain-affected match, Cullinan "chirped" at us all day. He never stopped abusing our batsmen, so much so that he managed to drop four catches in that innings. Our reaction was, "Who does this bloke think he is? He's been in Test cricket five minutes and he's carrying on like this."

Did Cullinan back up with some great batting? Hardly. He made a first ball duck in Melbourne and scores of 9, 2, 10 and 5 in the rest of the series. Craig McDermott got him in Melbourne and once in the Third Test in Adelaide. Steve Waugh got him in the other innings in Adelaide and I got him both times in the Second Test in Sydney. And yes we reminded him of how well he was going in the series. I had the wood over him in the one-day series as well and it is well recorded that he had no idea about my flipper, picking it or playing it. I found out later that Tony Greig went to South African coach Mike Procter to offer to advise Cullinan and found out that both the coach and the batsman did not even know what a flipper was or how it was supposed to come out of the hand.

Talk about naive sledging from Cullinan. If he had had the commonsense to stay quiet, look and learn — like most new Test players — he might have fared better in his first couple of years in Test cricket against Australia. Cullinan began to score good runs in 1996 and by the time Australia arrived in South Africa in 1997 he was the home side's leading batsman. In the months leading to that series he had even sought help from a sports psychologist about coping with the Aussies and my bowling — and, I suppose, with the backlash his sledging in Australia had caused him. Yet in 1997 I always felt I still had it over him, that he was unsure how to play me.

Although we did let Cullinan know about his cocky past we did not give him too hard a time because we did not have to — he didn't make that many runs when the series was in the balance. He was a better and improved player and did not have that much to say about himself. So we let him get on with his game. Having said that, I still feel very confident bowling to him.

The other South African with whom I clashed was young spinner Paul Adams and for much the same reason as Cullinan. I'd met Paul a few times before our 1997 tour and we'd discussed wrist spin bowling. In the nets at the start of the tour we chatted again and I told him that if he thought I could help him in any way, I'd be happy to talk to him towards the end of the series. He had heaps of potential and I was happy to help him — but only after the series. Then we were all surprised when Paul came out to bat in Johannesburg and carried on in a ridiculous way, pulling faces, poking his tongue out at the bowlers and strutting around as if he'd been a top

**Paul Adams, the South African spin bowler.
I thought his sense of humour was as strange
as his bowling action.**

Test bowler for years. Fair enough. If that behaviour put the Australian bowlers and fielders off their game then good luck to him, but by the same token if he struggled with the ball he would be reminded of that behaviour.

Mark Waugh spoke for all of us during Paul's innings in Johannesburg. "Listen champ, you better be able to bowl," Mark said to him.

History shows that Australia thrashed South Africa in that Test, came from behind to win a great Second Test and so take the series. Adams' figures in the First Test were 1 for 163. He bowled a little better in the Second Test and was replaced by off-spinner Pat Symcox for the Third. Enough said.

We thought Adams would have learned something after Johannesburg, but in the Second Test he again carried on foolishly and when, in a tense situation with his team 9 wickets down, he tried to reverse-sweep me again and was caught at first slip, I could not help laughing. What on earth was he trying to do, playing a shot like that? I'd never seen anything so silly in my life. Naturally I copped all the criticism for laughing at Adams. Fortunately, although I was criticised in the media, the great majority of the letters, faxes and messages I received after that incident said that Adams had carried on like an upstart and deserved what he got, because he was trying to take the mickey out of me and it backfired.

So much for the South Africans. Unfortunately other teams are not always as upfront and honest as the South Africans. The Englishmen do not say as much as we do, but some of them certainly do sledge. As well, their captain Mike Atherton likes to show his competitive spirit at times by saying the odd word.

The Pakistanis can be very aggressive and provocative. I've already talked about how Salim Malik, for one, had plenty to say while he was batting. In the field, the Pakistanis talk all day, often in Urdu, which can be annoying if you're not used to it. You know they're talking about you but you don't know what they're saying. Still, they only do it to put you off your game so it should be easy enough to ignore it and concentrate on what you're supposed to be doing.

The West Indies dominated world cricket — in Test matches anyway — for 15 years from the late 1970s. During that period they became used to winning and developed an obvious arrogance. Yet when any team played well against them and threatened to beat them they reacted sharply. Although I only played a few games against Desmond Haynes during his last visit to Australia in 1992–3, I heard all the stories about what Haynes got up to under his helmet at short leg. Although his words were directed at his bowlers, they were meant to intimidate batsmen. When you have an attack of four pacemen concentrating on bowling short of a length and lifting the ball into the rib area, there will always be a feeling of violence in the cricket. Haynes liked to remind batsmen about that, especially Australian captain Allan Border who for so many years was the wicket most highly prized by the West Indies. Through all those years AB never complained. He did not like the West Indies' attitude, but he saw it as part of a very tough game. It was only after he'd retired and the Australian team was being labelled yet again as "The Ugly Aussies" that AB finally spoke up in an article in *Inside Edge* cricket magazine. During his playing days AB never came out and said that so and so called me this or that or got stuck all game and put me down.

Remember the altercation between Steve Waugh and Curtly Ambrose in the Caribbean in 1995? Remember West Indies captain Richie Richardson had to drag Ambrose by the arm away from Steve? I don't remember anyone strongly criticising Ambrose for that ugly scene.

Ambrose got away with another nasty episode in his last over in Test cricket in Australia, in Perth in the Fifth Test this year. That over lasted 15 deliveries. There were nine no-balls and some of those were over the line by at least half a metre. I was batting with Andrew Bichel at the time and Australia was about to be beaten heavily. Ambrose was charging in as he knew it was his last chance to inflict some damage on an Australian team. Everything was short and lifting on a difficult, cracked pitch, with two lower order batsmen at the crease. Was Ambrose trying to hit Andrew and me? You can make up your own mind on that one. The crowd was jeering and the atmosphere out there was electric, but there was no way Andy and I were going to concede ground. We both decided that at times we would charge and try to belt Ambrose around the WACA. We did for a while too although not every ball. Andy had to turn his back on one lifter and take it in the middle of his back. But both of us were determined not to give an inch to Ambrose, a player who had said very little to Australian cricketers throughout his career. I have never played against a more remote person than Ambrose. He was popular with his teammates and was supposed to be the life of the party but to any opponents he was a threatening presence, off the field as well as on it.

In recent years the ICC match referees have kept a lid on behaviour and I agree with that, with one proviso. The game still needs its characters. As long as players are allowed to express themselves and show some emotion within reason out on the field, the crowds will be entertained and the matches will maintain that atmosphere of tension and drama that every Test match should provide. It will always be a fine line between the two.

STEVE SIEWERT/THE FAIRFAX PHOTO LIBRARY

Facing the West Indies on one of the fastest pitches in the world.
Final Test at the WACA, 1993, when Curtly Ambrose blitzed us.

STEVE CUFF/SPORTSEXPOSURE

**No needle here — a hat-trick with a difference,
with umpire Dickie Bird.**

Equally television coverage has been great for the modern game. The danger with it in this area of player behaviour is that occasionally the cameras tend to follow players with a reputation for "sledging" and they miss others who are just as guilty. That can give the impression that there is more aggro going on in the middle than is really the case. As a result some individuals are hard done by. The cameras are important to the game and the public and, in the end, if there is an incident out in the middle they have to show it. That's life for an international cricketer and we have to cope with it.

The Brotherhood of Spin

An interesting moment in my international career happened in a house in Pakistan, not on the field at Lord's or the Melbourne Cricket Ground. It was on the 1994 tour to Pakistan and I was in a house with the manager of the great Pakistani leg-spinner Abdul Qadir. I'd seen a little of Qadir bowling, though not much. But I did know that for nearly a decade he was by far the best of a very small group of wrist spinners playing international cricket. Word reached me that Qadir enjoyed my bowling and would be happy to have a chat about spin bowling if I could find the time. A meeting was arranged and soon enough I found myself sitting on the carpet in that house flicking flippers, toppies and wrong'uns back and forth with a truly great leg-spinner.

Qadir was still playing first-class cricket in Pakistan that season and many locals thought he should have been playing in the Test series. He was not selected, but was certainly happy to swap ideas with and offer advice to me. Qadir had a whippy, springy action on which his successor as Pakistan's leggie, Mushtaq Ahmed, has based his action. And fair enough too. Qadir's action was tremendous, good for leg-spin bowling and entertaining for crowds because of the way he would twirl the ball in his hands before winding up and starting his skipping run to the crease. He had a great leg-spinner and a great wrong'un, whereas my bowling is based on a big-spinning leggie, top spinners and my flipper. Qadir was keen to see how I bowled my flipper and in return he showed me how he bowled his wrong'un. We got on well and it was a thrill to meet the man who virtually single-handedly had kept leg-spin bowling alive throughout a decade or so dominated by great pace bowlers.

From the late 1970s through most of the 1980s wrist spin was in decline. It was out of fashion and looked like fading from the game. Apart from Qadir, the best bowlers of that era were pacemen: Dennis Lillee and Jeff Thomson from Australia, the great West Indians, Malcolm Marshall, Andy Roberts, Michael Holding, Joel Garner, New Zealand's Richard Hadlee, Bob Willis and Ian Botham from England, Pakistan's Imran Khan and India's Kapil Dev. Pace had dominated for so long that a generation of kids had grown up bowling as fast as they could in their backyards, in their school playgrounds and at their club nets. A kid had to be mad to try to become a wrist spinner. For a start it is such a difficult craft that a kid will soon give it up unless he or she receives special coaching and lots of encouragement. As well, most captains did not know how to use a spinner, especially a wrist spinner. The emphasis was on pace and if not that medium-pace. Most captains did not know how to set proper fields for spinners nor how to use them as wicket-takers. When the time came to rest their fast bowlers captains turned to medium-pacers to tie an end down until the quicks could return. Unless it was straight out pace, the cricket was defensive. As well, most matches were played on a limited-overs basis, even first grade in the capital cities where 100 overs was the maximum for the first innings. It sounds like a lot of overs, but it was the Les Stillman theory: attack with the new ball then tighten things up for the rest of the day. It was 50-over cricket doubled in length. Captains were reluctant to risk bowling a wrist spinner and so there were few young ones coming through.

I was lucky to see leg-spin at my club when I was young and then to have people like Victoria's under-age selectors, then Jim Higgs, Terry Jenner and Jack Potter to give me the encouragement I needed in those early years. At least the people involved in representative cricket in Australia — from under-15 through to the Test selectors, were always on the look-out for promising young spinners, especially wrist spinners. Leggies had served Australia well for years and years — people like Arthur Mailey, Clarrie Grimmett, Bill O'Reilly and Richie Benaud had been great bowlers and Australian cricket had not forgotten how destructive a good leg-spinner could be. English batsmen always struggled against wrist spinners as did New Zealanders, West Indians and South Africans. These days England play the quicks better. Pakistan and India had always had wonderful spin bowlers so their batsmen grew up on spin. They were so-called better players of spin than batsmen from other countries, but even so good spinners still took wickets against teams from the subcontinent. I'm sure that if I'd been born in England, New Zealand, South Africa or the West Indies I wouldn't have received the encouragement I did receive in Australia and so would not have gone as far in the game as I have. Thanks.

To look around the world now and see England playing two spinners at last — both finger spinners but still an attacking move — as well as Sri Lanka, Pakistan, India, Zimbabwe and South Africa all picking a specialist spinner, if not two is exciting and very good for the game. A lot of those spinners are only young and that should mean that spin will at least hold its own for quite a while, if not come to dominate bowling through the 1990s and into the next century. And that pattern is seen in one-day cricket, not just Test cricket. People have realised that good spinners can confuse and therefore slow down batsmen in one-day cricket. Remember when slower balls were first bowled by Steve Waugh and Simon O'Donnell? A spinner does the same thing. Spinners played a large and successful part in the World Cup on the subcontinent in 1996 and long may that continue.

If I have had a small part to play in helping spin bowling return to a prominent place in the game then I'm a happy man. Certainly judging from the number of letters I receive from kids asking for a few tips, we'll be seeing good spinners for a long time yet. It was that amount of mail which gave me the idea of developing a spinner's kit which included a small ball with the finger positions for several deliveries marked. People seemed to enjoy it and I'm hoping to produce another one soon with a few more of my repertoire.

In England in 1993, my first Ashes tour, it was tremendous and very satisfying for me to see so many kids flicking balls out of the back of their hands as they played on the country grounds during breaks in play in our tour games. I received lots of fan mail on that tour as well and it would be great for world cricket and England cricket if the Poms found a few good young wrist spinners in the future. Spinners add variety and entertainment to the game. Spectators love watching spinners, just as they love watching great fast bowlers. Spinners increase over rates and offer batsmen the chance to play a wider range of shots than they can to pace bowlers. With a good spinner bowling to a good batsman who is prepared to use his feet, you have one of cricket's best and most thrilling contests. World cricket is better for having spin bowling back to a position of prominence. Sixes, stumpings, and so on. Or maybe I'm just biased.

Perhaps because spinners were neglected for so many years, the current bunch of international spinners are quite close. Naturally enough I'm very good mates with the other Australian spinners. Some of the most enjoyable times I've had on a cricket field were in England in 1993 bowling at the other end to Tim May. 'Maysie' is a very funny bloke with a sharp, dry sense of humour. When you add that to his ability to find every possible

CRAIG GOLDING/THE FAIRFAX PHOTO LIBRARY

MARK RAY

LEFT & ABOVE: With Tim May, the off-spinner. We were a team on the 1993 Ashes tour but in 1994-5 it was our last-ditch batting that stopped England winning a Test at the SCG.

way to have accidents and injure himself, you have a most entertaining teammate. As well, I believed that we bowled well together. I was a better bowler for having Maysie working away at the other end and that pairing worked best on that 1993 Ashes tour. I was disappointed Maysie did not play on for longer, but he had come to the end of the line I suppose. These days we're involved together in the newly formed Australian Cricketers' Association and hopefully that organisation will look after the needs of Australia's first-class cricketers as the game becomes more professional and so more demanding.

As well as working closely with Tim May and Michael Bevan, Australia's new chinaman discovery, I have swapped tactics, grips and technical ideas with most of the international spinners going round. Zimbabwe's Paul Strang is an excellent leg-spinner as well as a lovely bloke. If Paul were playing for a stronger team and being seen more he'd be a superstar. He and I have had plenty of conversations about bowling. The same goes for Anil Kumble. We've swapped ideas over a meal in India and he's a fine bowler, although very different in style to me. I'm sure he would love to play more Test cricket instead of the one-day series the Indian administrators seem to prefer.

A couple of years ago I suggested to Mushtaq Ahmed that he needed to lower his bowling arm a little to get more leg-spin. He has a great wrong'un but batsmen around the world had worked him out and had begun playing him like an off-spinner because they knew he did not turn his leg-break much. Mushie took my advice and we worked on it in the nets at the MCG. Then, during our Test series in Australia in 1995–6, he started turning his

BEN RADFORD/ALL SPORT

Australia played two leg spinners against England in the Fourth Test in Adelaide, 1995. Peter McIntyre and I were the spin twins.

leggie more. All of a sudden the wickets started coming and a few of my teammates told me I should take it easy on this businesss of helping the opposition. But as players like Dennis Lillee and Ian Chappell always say, if a player from one country helps a player from another improve his game world cricket is that much better. I haven't had much to do with Mushie's teammate Saqlain Mushtaq, mainly because he is an off-spinner, but it is obvious that he is already an outstanding bowler.

Before I became established as an international bowler I was good friends with most spin bowlers around Australia. Like the international fraternity, spinners in the state teams in Australia tend to make friends with each other even if it's only to catch up after a day's play for a beer and a whinge about batsmen or flat pitches. I've already talked about what an influence Greg Matthews was on my Test career at a crucial early stage. Although he was always supportive of younger spin bowlers, he used to give them a harsh introduction to first-class cricket (and still does), bowling a bouncer as fast as he can, saying, "Welcome to the big league!" Paul Jackson, a left-arm orthodox bowler, and Peter McIntyre, a leg-spinner who has played Test cricket for Australia, were in the Victorian team in the years just before I was selected, before they both moved interstate to receive more opportunities.

Unless something very important crops up, I go across to Adelaide once a winter for the Academy's spin bowling week. Spinners from all over Australia gather to receive coaching from people like Terry Jenner, Ashley Mallett and Kerry O'Keeffe. I really enjoy mixing with the younger guys, swapping ideas, showing them a few tricks and generally encouraging them to stick with spin bowling. The Australian Cricket Board has had a pace bowling program going for several years now with Dennis Lillee as the main coach. Although the ACB has organised a few spin clinics I think it could be put on a more formal and regular footing as with the Pace Australia program. It is harder to find the next good Test spinner than the next quick because in general there are fewer kids bowling spin, even now that a revival is under way. More work in promoting and coaching spin bowling will help Australian cricket stay on top of the world.

Life on the Road

By the end of Australia's very successful tour to South Africa in early 1997, I had had enough of life on the road and was getting desperate for a rest, for a few weeks at home. It had been a long summer for the Australian team. Since the previous November we'd played eight Tests — five against the West Indies and three against South Africa, two of the best teams in the world — as well as 14 one-day internationals. In the two months before our home season began there had been a one-day tournament in Sri Lanka then a one-off Test and a one-day series in India. After the tour to South Africa we had three weeks at home before heading to England for six Tests, three one-day internationals and numerous tour games over three and a half months. After England, there were to be six Tests at home against New Zealand and South Africa plus a minimum of seven one-day matches, a short tour to New Zealand, then a three-Test tour of India with a one-day series as well.

In those 21 months we will have played 24 Tests and many more one-day internationals. We'll have played in five countries on five continents, travelled thousands and thousands of miles and stayed in too many hotels to remember. Life on the road for an international cricketer is very tough these days and the grind takes its toll — on your mind as well as your body.

It sounds great to be in South Africa or India playing cricket, but really we don't see much of these places. Generally what we see is airport, plane, bus, hotel, cricket ground, hotel, cricket ground, bus, airport, plane, airport, bus, hotel, cricket ground and on and on. I know we are well paid for this and we know what to expect. I'm not whingeing, but I am saying that being well paid for it does not mean you are suddenly going to have lots of fun or more spare time. We are well paid for it because we work hard.

When we are in places where there is political tension — and that happens more and more these days — we end up spending all our time at the ground or the hotel because we cannot go out at night. Hotels are the same wherever you are and in the end you start to go a little stir crazy stuck in a hotel with nothing much to do to pass the time between training sessions and matches. Steve Waugh reckons that the tour to Sri Lanka in '96 was the worst he had ever been on because we weren't allowed to leave the hotel due to the political trouble there at the time. Even in peaceful countries we do not have much time for sightseeing. You can come back from a tour to a fascinating country and struggle to tell people anything original about what you saw. In nine weeks in South Africa we had only three or four days free of travel, training, official functions or playing. To have won both the Test series and the one-day series against a very good team was an outstanding achievement, especially because the tour came at the end of such a long, tough road. I think the Australian team showed how determined and proud we are by doing so well in South Africa in 1997.

In season '96–7, while I was travelling around Australia and South Africa my wife Simone was at home going through her first pregnancy. When the baby was born where was I? On the other side of the world, playing cricket somewhere in England. I'm certainly not the first Australian cricketer to have that experience and I won't be the last. I realise that thousands

Cooking up a storm during the Boxing Day Test against the West Indies in 1996. Well, maybe it was a toasted cheese sandwich!

of people would give their right arms to be travelling the world playing cricket for their country. It gives you the opportunity to meet fascinating people and hopefully plan a good future after cricket. A lot of people I meet along the way say that to me. But equally there are plenty of people who tell me they would not want to be in my shoes. At times I feel like swapping with the guy who says he'd love to do what I do. I could fade off into the distance and live a more private life. Trouble is I'd miss the game, the actual cricket and the challenges it presents before too long, as well as the celebrations with the boys when we've won a Test match.

People sometimes wonder why Australian cricketers play so much golf on tour instead of sightseeing. Firstly in most countries we cannot play the tourist like other people. We are recognised and so people want to talk to us, get autographs, have their photos taken with us. When we are away from the game, the nets and the hotel for a brief while, the last thing we want is to be reminded about cricket. Sometimes we just need to get away from the game completely to refresh our minds. Playing golf is a way of getting rid of frustrations — or at least directing them on to our golf — and also getting away from that spotlight. For a few hours on a beautiful golf course we can forget about the pressures and just be ourselves. The public are great and I love them, but it is important to have some time to ourselves, which we can get on a golf course, and I think that deep down that is why so many of us end up playing golf instead of going sightseeing. My partner at the moment is Greg Blewett, who plays off 4, and my handicap (besides my swing) is 14. So we aren't a bad team. The most enjoyable part of playing golf these days is when we view Junior Waugh's money.

Different players handle touring life in different ways. Quite often I prefer to either play golf, maybe tennis, or just stay in my hotel room. I might watch television, listen to some music or even take the phone off the hook and have a few extra hours sleep. Most bowlers, especially the fast men, tend to spend their free time relaxing, either in their hotel room or at the swimming pool. One of my closest friends and a great Australian cricketer, Merv Hughes, said you should never spoil a rest day, you must feel good. But if you've ever seen Merv play golf you'd understand why he'd rather put his feet up. Steve Waugh likes to get out and about as much as he can. He usually has a few ideas on each tour about things he wants to do or see or people he wants to meet. During the World Cup he made an early morning call on Mother Theresa in Calcutta. Stephen will load his camera and off he goes, while I'll probably be back in my hotel room hibernating. No wonder cricketers call their hotel rooms "the bat cave".

STEPHEN MUNDAY/ALL SPORT

**Grooving the golf swing at Moorpark, Ashes tour 1993.
It's a way to forget about the pressures of cricket.**

Greg Matthews and Michael Whitney used to love getting out of the hotel and seeing something of the lives and customs of the people. Whit had been a world traveller before he played for Australia and he couldn't resist that urge to get out and see something of the country. Whit is an outgoing guy who has a knack of meeting and charming people. For others who aren't quite like that, sightseeing and meeting people can be tiring and they tend to hang back at the hotel. Each to his own.

Of course sightseeing can depend on where you are. In Pakistan there just isn't that much to do at night or see during the day. Restaurants are rare so hotel life dominates. In Pakistan in 1994 we ran our own casino nights, had heaps of videos and music. We basically entertained ourselves in a team room at the hotel. India and Sri Lanka offer more to see and do although the crowds of fans — hundreds and hundreds — can keep you in the hotel. There is no shortage of attractions in the Caribbean and South Africa and no shortage of willing hosts, people who are involved in local cricket or who just contact our manager and offer the team a boat for a day's fishing or a helicopter flight over beautiful Cape Town. Brian Lara showed me a few places in the Caribbean in 1995 and Brian McMillan organised a boat to take a few of the Aussies fishing off Cape Town. Mark Taylor, Matthew Elliott and Geoff Marsh are the keenest fishermen in our squad.

Once you've toured a few times with a team you learn the basic rules. In the Australian team no one is safe from copping it from the rest. We all have our foibles and nothing escapes your teammates. We can all cop that, but also we know what it can be like if the guys won't leave you alone or repeat the same joke until you've had enough. At times we all feel like that and it is important for the rest of the team to spot that time and ease off that player. Although I have to admit that there are also days when his teammates know a player has got out of bed on the wrong side and is not in a good mood. Occasionally the other players will decide to goad him just to see how far they can go before he cracks. It seems a bit cruel but usually once the player has cracked and spat the dummy he feels better for it. There's no place in the Aussie side for anyone who is a bit sensitive.

In every team that stays in hotels, there is always the player no one wants to share a room with. It used to be Tim May in our team because of his snoring. It was horrendous. No matter what you threw at him or what techniques he tried, Maysie's snoring was hard to handle. At the moment we don't have anyone who is a nightmare to share with, although Glenn McGrath can be a worry. Glenn grew up on a farm and still loves knives and guns. If

**Dog-tired with Michael Slater on a flight
from Melbourne to Sydney in 1993.**

he is in one of his mischievous moods you never know what he's going to do. In any group of people living together you'll have the tidy, fussy ones and the messy ones. Craig McDermott used to be amazingly tidy and could get upset if he had to share with messy guys like Steve Waugh or myself. It is one of the manager's jobs to sort our roommates on a tour so that the problems are kept to a minimum. For the past couple of seasons in Australia and in Test matches overseas we have been rooming separately before and during Test matches. This has worked really well because the nerves and tension associated with a Test affect different people in different ways. Having a room of your own allows you to do what you prefer without disturbing anyone else.

It has been said many times before, but there is no doubt the best tour of all is an Ashes tour. England is similar to Australia in so many ways and the people there always make an Australian team feel welcome. Most of any Australian squad will have played cricket in England — league cricket or, more and more these days, county cricket. We all have plenty of friends in England and catching up with them is one of the delights of an Ashes tour. Although in England some of the hotel rooms can be pretty small, we have the compensation of travelling in a team bus. We don't fly internally as we do in most other countries, including at home every summer. The bus is a place where team morale builds strongly. These days we have television, videos, music, food, couches for stretching out — everything we need while we're moving from venue to venue and match to match.

International cricket is very popular these days and is shown on free-to-air or pay television for hours and hours. This is great for the game but it does mean that the spotlight is on the players much more than it was in the past. I know this is part of the job and it does lead to opportunities after cricket, but cricketers are human too and the spotlight and the pressures that come with the job do get to all the players. At times it feels like the cameras and the public are watching your every move. I mean people constantly criticise Mark Taylor because he chews gum so much on the field or Steve Waugh because he doesn't smile enough. At times I feel trapped by all this. It is no wonder some of us occasionally blow our tops in tense situations on the field. It's a wonder it does not happen more often.

I know we are role models for kids and we're aware of our wider responsibilities to the game and the country we represent, but like every other person we have days when we are tired or get out of the wrong side of the bed. The trouble is that when that happens to most people they let fly in the kitchen at home or in the office in front of half a dozen people. But when we do it, chances are we will be in the middle of a crowded cricket ground with television cameras beaming our every move into living rooms all over the world. If not, we might be on a plane or in a hotel lobby, somewhere in uniform in view of the public. One step out of line and we're in trouble. Sometimes you feel like you have no escape, that everything you do is watched, analysed and often criticised. It's part of the game and in the end we have to learn to deal with it the best way we can.

On the field, I play it hard. I appeal aggressively or, as some people say, arrogantly. I'm not arrogant. I have confidence in my ability. Yes, I'm emotional about my cricket. I'm competitive and aggressive. I have to be. I'm a bowler and I'm there to dismiss batsmen. That's what I'm paid to do. But I'm not arrogant. I always enjoy a beer and a chat with opponents after play and I've not heard of any opponents complaining about me as a person. I know I lost control in Johannesburg in 1994, but I've already explained the background to that. That mistake is the only thing I'd like to take back from my whole career. I'll stand by everything else. And what some people forget is that we are different off the field. To put it simply, I'm a bit like Jeckle and Hyde. Off the field I'm laidback, on the field I'm super competitive and aggressive and sometimes go too far. But I'm an emotional cricketer and who wants robots?

Fame and All That Jazz

We are not sure why, but his teammates have noticed that Mark Waugh often receives gifts of flowers from his fans; flowers and chocolates. Maybe that's partly why Mike Whitney and Greg Matthews nicknamed Mark 'Pretty' as in 'Pretty Boy'. Most international cricketers are well known and receive plenty of mail, some of it interesting, some of it not. Usually the letters contain photographs or cards to sign, requests for advice on batting or bowling and occasionally a request to be a guest at a wedding or a surprise birthday party. I once received a pair of knickers in the mail, but they're difficult to sign. I try to answer all letters and my wife Simone has been a great help in this. Sadly some players also receive hate mail. Once I spot that sort of letter I throw it away. There is not much you can do about it. I learnt a few years ago that not everyone will like you and the reasons may vary from the way you walk to the way you appeal, the fact that you wear an earring or your hairstyle. Often it is simply the fact that some people are jealous of anyone who is successful. Becoming a cricketer has its plusses and minuses — like anything else — and hate mail is one of the negatives.

A potential positive can be the advice some people offer in letters. One guy from Perth sent me a cardboard pyramid which I was to assemble then put my injured finger under for treatment. He swore that the pyramid treatment would help my finger to heal after the surgery I'd had on it. I have to admit I never tried the pyramid, but I appreciated the thought, as I do whenever my fans offer advice or constructive criticism.

I learned during my early career that you cannot please everyone. Some people will love you and others will hate you. The best thing you can do is be yourself. Some people will approve; others won't. I'm lucky that the majority of people like the way I play cricket and conduct myself.

Another negative occurs when you are seen by the media doing something that a minority of people do not like. A classic example happened to me during the Test against Pakistan in Brisbane in November 1995.

Australia won the Test and I was man of the match. When I came off the field, I grabbed a drink and went to a press and television conference, which the Australian Cricket Board requires us to do. That took about an hour. While my teammates were celebrating a great victory I was doing the right thing by the media. The boys were waiting for me so we could sing 'Underneath the Southern Cross' — something we do after every Test victory.

After the press guys had finished with me I headed towards the dressingroom when Patrick Keane, the ACB's media officer, said I had one more radio interview to do in a back room out of the way of the traffic outside the dressingrooms. I told Patrick that was fine as long as I could grab my cigarettes and another drink. Soon enough I was doing the interview with no one else around. I lit up a cigarette and noticed a camera flash go off. I turned around to see News Limited photographer Trent Parke. Trent was on the tour for the first time and I thought he would realise that I was not smoking in public view but in private. I wouldn't have lit up had the public been there or I'd known there were cameras on me.

I thought nothing more about the picture until all hell broke loose a day or two later when Sydney's *Daily Telegraph* and other News Limited papers around the country used it prominently. Trent had sent the picture down the phone line to his paper and once they had seen it he had no chance of getting them to agree not to use it. Even though I was doing something in private that might not be good for my fitness but is still legal, the *Telegraph* attacked me for setting a bad example to kids. I was annoyed with the way they treated me and Trent was upset as he had made a mistake early in his first tour.

People from all over the country started jumping on their high horses and criticising me for irresponsibility. Two people quick to pounce were Melbourne footballer Garry Lyon and football manager Ricky Nixon. When Garry, who is a great bloke, finally realised the full circumstances, that I had been on my own in a back room underneath the grandstand talking on radio to one journalist, he wrote to me to apologise. But Nixon didn't really admit he had jumped to the wrong conclusion without knowing the full facts. The episode upset me but it also taught me that I have to watch what I'm doing, wearing and saying just about all the time.

Signing autographs is a major part of a cricketer's life. The game attracts collectors — people who want players to sign bats, photographs, t-shirts and occasionally parts of their anatomies. The TV cameras once caught me signing a woman's breast during a one-day game in Sydney and a press photographer caught me signing a young lady's upper leg in Durban, South

Africa on the 1997 tour. The lady had come over to the fence where I was fielding and asked for an autograph. She then lifted her dress and pointed to a spot on her … well, upper leg, where she wanted my signature. Never one to knock back a request for an autograph, I obliged. My wife was not impressed when she saw the photo in a Melbourne paper the next day. Being a long way from the action and pregnant made it worse.

I still remember being a kid lining up to get the autographs of my heroes, especially Hawthorn footballer Peter Knights. I know the thrill of being close to one of your heroes and watching him as he signs your book, maybe even asks you how you are going. I try to sign for every autograph-seeker who asks politely. The two occasions when I've had time but refused to sign was during the Third Test at Centurion Park in Pretoria and at a one-day international at the Wanderers in Johannesburg towards the end of the 1997 tour to South Africa. Those crowds had booed me and the team through those games then waited for me after play expecting me to sign autographs for them. Sorry, but I could not do it. I know some of them might only have booed to put me off my bowling and I realise that sometimes I bring this on myself by my actions on the field, but I felt those crowds had been a little unpleasant and I was not going to reward them for it. The difficult aspect was that I felt sorry for the kids; but I was really angry.

The one major drawback on a tour of England is the publicity from the tabloid newspapers. They are quite happy to send reporters or photographers "undercover" to grab some juicy gossip or manufacture a scandal. During the 1993 Ashes tour Merv Hughes, myself and our girlfriends were heading off in a car to a team dinner outside of the city we were playing in at the time. After a while we noticed a car following us and we became suspicious. At a set of traffic lights, I jumped out to check on this guy. I noticed a camera and flash on the front seat beside him and told him we were "off duty" and to stop following us.

"Come on, mate," he said. "Just a quick photo and I'll leave you alone."

I repeated that we were trying to enjoy a private night out and wanted to be left alone. The photographer continued following us until Merv stopped our car and went over and gave this guy a serve. He dropped off then, but it was a warning to us about the extent the tabloids would go to get a different picture.

Of course many of the things that happen to an international cricketer are terrific. So many people in politics, music and business love cricket that you end up meeting some fascinating people. The Farriss brothers in INXS love their cricket and we've met them on a few occasions. I've met Elton

John once and no doubt will see him again soon. He's a tremendous supporter of all cricket and has often shouted a great meal to the Australian players and their wives and girlfriends. Every cricketer who plays a Test at Lord's meets the Queen, but Allan Border and I actually had a good chat with Princess Diana at a charity lunch in Sydney in October 1996. She was charming and followed cricket. She said her sons loved the game. Two other famous women I've met are the supermodels Helena Christiansen and Claudia Schiffer. Helena and I actually shared a catwalk one day in Melbourne. It was my first experience modelling like that and I didn't realise how long a catwalk is. I think from memory it was 30 metres. I was told that while I was walking down the catwalk I was to undo the buttons of my jacket one at a time, and when I reached the end whip open the jacket and do a spin. But I forgot to undo the last button and I when I got to the end I couldn't get my jacket off. Another embarrassing trap for beginners.

Through my visits to Crown Casino in Melbourne I've met the owners, Lloyd Williams and Ron Walker, and through my involvement with Channel Nine I've met Kerry and James Packer. Lloyd and I play quite a lot of golf together and we've become good mates. As well, through my involvement with Nike I've met Michael Jordan and Andre Agassi — both legends of world sport. Jordan was impressive. He'd seen a little cricket and Aussie Rules on television in the UK. We gave him a footy as a gift and I couldn't help wondering how well he'd go at centre half-forward for St Kilda.

Meeting such famous people and visiting some special places is great fun. But it is the same as making good money. It's enjoyable but nothing beats playing in the Australian cricket team, especially one that is winning. The only reason I've met these people is because of my cricket. Without that it's back to work, somewhere. As long as I'm enjoying my cricket I'll be happy. Everything will take care of itself if your cricket is going well. All of this would mean nothing if I was dropped from the Test side or if my spinning finger had not recovered from that operation. If I had to keep one part of my life and drop the rest (excluding family, of course), I'd keep the cricket. No doubt about it.

NIKE PUBLICITY

'Fame' has its finer moments. My deal with Nike gave me the chance
to meet one of world sport's shining stars, Michael Jordan.

The Poms

In any day's play in a Test match, there is one crucial, tough period that decides who wins that day's cricket. That period is the one where a batting team loses a wicket which might end an important partnership or suffers a mini collapse when it loses three or four quick wickets and the back of the innings is broken. For a bowling team, that decisive moment might be when a new batsman is in and you bowl to his weakness, find an edge only for the catch to be dropped. It could be Steve Waugh, the toughest wicket to take in the world at present. If a team drops Steve before he's reached double figures, they will probably pay a heavy price. Often after a mistake like that the balance of play swings. The bowlers lose spirit and confidence, the fielders drop their heads and all of a sudden the two batsmen have added 50 and are looking comfortable. It can come down to that — a split second where a player might freeze under pressure or not be concentrating in the slips, for example, and bang the day's play — maybe the match — is lost.

In the two Ashes series I've played in —1993 in England and 1994–5 at home — the Australian team has won all but two or three of those tight moments in each day's play. England beat us in the Sixth Test at the Oval in 1993 and in the Fourth in Adelaide in early 1995 and, although we had already won the series and had eased off psychologically, England did play tougher, more adventurous cricket in both those games. That's one reason why they won, yet they don't seem to have learned from those games. Most of the time they have doubted themselves at the crucial moments. I'm not sure whether it's their lack of genuine confidence, cautious leadership or just their not knowing how to win, but it's worth remembering how they won both those Tests against us.

At the Oval, on a fast bouncy pitch, it was their fastest bowler who did the damage. If Devon Malcolm had been an Australian he might have played many more Test matches. If he'd played most games he would have been used as a strike bowler. Devon can be very quick and nasty to handle, yet

England seemed to use him in long spells as if he were a stock bowler. It was crazy and it seemed to ruin his career. At the Oval in 1993, Devon let loose and won England the game. Admittedly his form was sometimes erratic, but I'm sure he never felt comfortable in the team. Even when he had won England a Test, he probably never felt secure about his position nor, when he played a stretch of games, certain about his role. When England used him as a strike bowler — told him he'd be bowling in four-over spells and that he could charge in and let rip — he did the job very well. In both those games where England beat us, Devon did exactly that. Remember him charging in from the Bradman Stand end in Adelaide and causing mayhem in our second innings? And he was allowed to do that because of an attacking, rearguard innings the day before from Phil DeFreitas who played to his potential with the bat then, his confidence on a high, bowled well in support of Devon the next day. Amazing how quickly your confidence can grow if you've taken a risk, backed yourself, and it has come off. England do not play like that often enough. When the crunch comes and we see they are not game to grab the advantage we'll take it every time.

Perhaps that proves that the English side is soft. Certainly it's obvious they need to start winning more of the tougher moments. In the past few series, England have played well when they've felt comfortable. As soon as a tough moment comes along, they've crumbled — they've lost two or three quick wickets or they haven't been able to take the important wicket. Perhaps it is about really wanting to represent your country, and to do well out of personal pride which comes from deep, deep down. Too many England players enjoy playing for their country without it being a life-or-death situation. If you look at the top players in the world they really want to do well for their country. They don't care about anything more than playing at their best and crushing the opposition, trying to nail them every time. I don't think England players have had that killer instinct. I think deep down they have been soft. When the situation has turned against them they haven't been able to find that extra 5 or 10 per cent to lift, like Ian Botham did so often. Mike Atherton and Darren Gough are two exceptions and that's why Goughie should be in every England team as long as he's fit. He never gives up and, like Atherton, he has guts and pride.

When I became captain of Victoria for the 1996–7 season, John Scholes, the coach, and I talked about getting the team to do all the 'one-percenters', the little things that add up. It might only be ringing your roommate and telling him to hurry up if you realise he's running late for the team bus. A small thing, but it counts. Other examples are backing up the throws in the field as a habit, making every net session constructive, showing the guys how important it is to be dressed properly, digging deep for your teammates, setting your goals high rather then settling for second best. The Australian team learned to do that under Allan Border and continues to do it now. The best comment I've heard about this sort of thing is that when you have reached the Number 1 spot you have to keep training like you are Number 2. Set high standards and keep pushing yourself. In many areas of English cricket, the one percenters are not seen as important and that sort of attitude eventually shows on the scoreboard.

Since Ian Botham retired England have only occasionally been able to grab the initiative in Test matches. Botham used to do it for them — and Bob Willis and David Gower. Gower was often criticised for getting out softly but often he did the job for England. And when he didn't he was always trying to do something, to take the initiative away from the opposition. One of England's problems since Botham retired is that they've spent so much time looking for the next Botham. Players like that don't come along that often. England have been looking for their next saviour, their next miracle worker, instead of making sure that the players who've been there have improved as cricketers and have learnt how to play good, tough Test cricket.

Graeme Hick is a classic example of a talented England player who has not been able to handle the constant pressure of Test cricket. For whatever reason, Hick hasn't harnessed his natural ability to lift those extra cogs to succeed in Test cricket. He is good enough, no doubt. He has heaps of talent, but Test cricket is played in the head as much as on the pitch and that was where Hick seemed to fall down. Maybe he had played too many easy county games against ordinary bowlers on flat pitches and had forgotten how tough the game could be, even for very good players. There have been plenty of other England players not able to cope consistently with Test cricket, but Hick is probably the most talented. Maybe finding out why Hick faded would help England stop that sort of thing happening to the next generation of talented cricketers.

Another thing which makes it hard for the England team to do well consistently is that the whole country — the press, supporters and officials — are always looking for reasons to criticise their team. Admittedly the England team doesn't help its cause by playing poorly, but the people around them rarely look for positives. It seems to me that English people tend to dwell on the negatives. It runs through their whole game. They have to be more positive about their game, their national team and their outlook. When

Getting ready for battle in England in 1997. The wet early summer threatened to make our Ashes defence a nightmare.

England plays a bad game, everyone says, "Here we go again. Same old story." It would be better if people said, "Right, we've played badly so what went wrong and what can we do to improve in the next game?" Personal and national pride has to come into it, but at a deep level, not just in pleasant-sounding words. People have to think of the national cap, the great history of English Test cricket, the people who have played before them, and then work out ways to improve.

That is what Australia did when Allan Border took over the captaincy in tough times during the mid-1980s. Faced with major problems, the selectors decided to search for players with the right temperaments — Boon, Waugh, Jones, Hughes, McDermott — then tell them that if they worked hard and showed that they wanted to give everything for the baggy green cap the selectors would stick by them. It was a long-term policy and it worked brilliantly. The Australian Cricket Board also looked to the long-term and set up the Cricket Academy which now produces young players who are further along the road to first-class cricket than they would otherwise have been. Through the Academy a generation of ex-players — like Ian Chappell, Terry Jenner, Dennis Lillee and, of course, chief coach Rod Marsh — has come back to bring the younger players on towards being tough, well-educated first-class players. England has to do something similar. It is time now for the Poms to really stand up. They can't just sit there and say, "It would be nice if England were playing well, but we can't really expect too much." They just can't continue to set low standards. You have to expect the best and work towards achieving it.

One of the things that makes the job of improving standards in English cricket difficult is that the counties have such good followings. That should be a positive but it's not. It means they are reluctant to change their system. In 1993 I was amazed that England's Test bowlers were rarely rested by their counties between Tests and often struggled to even get to Test practice in reasonable shape. Some of them would have to drive the length of England along crowded motorways from a county game to make it to practice the day before a Test match. They should not have to do that. If the counties refuse to rest them then the Test selectors should be able to make them do it. In 1997 the newly formed England and Wales Cricket Board gave the selectors the right to order the counties to rest players. In the end, the national team is the most important. If it is playing well, kids will want to play cricket instead of another major sport.

From what I've seen, I think there should be fewer county teams so that there are more good players per team. That would raise the standard, because if you have better players playing against each other all the time then the standard will naturally be higher. It would also reduce the number of games so that players could have some time to rest and recharge their batteries. Perhaps the county set-up could use a draft system as we have in Australian football where the best young players are selected from a talent pool to go to certain clubs, in this case counties. That would help even the competition and ensure good matches. At the moment we are lucky in Australia because we have a lot of depth. Think of the players who did not make the 1997 Ashes squad: Stuart Law, Matthew Hayden, Damien Martyn and Darren Lehmann. Even Paul Reiffel was only called up after Andrew Bichel was injured. With that sort of depth, our Sheffield Shield competition does not drop in standard too much when the top players are away on international duty. I don't think England have that sort of depth so they can't afford to see the standard of county cricket drop further when the Test players are busy elsewhere. Fewer county games — though probably still more than the 11 we usually play in Australia each season — would mean that the counties could field their international players more often and would avoid the situation where players feel jaded. Instead they would feel fresh and raring to go. And the seconds players would have to earn their stripes to get a game in the firsts, rather than filling in so often for weary senior players.

**Allan Border scored a few hundreds in the backyard at Mum's.
When I was young 'AB' was one of my favourite 'pretend' players — how
could I ever have dreamt that one day he'd be my captain?**

Desmond Haynes. He's one of the openers in my World XII. He never lacked flair or confidence, and when he was 'in' there something cold-blooded and clinical about the way he gathered runs.

Mark Waugh is in my 'other' World XII — the players I consider to be the best in the world today. 'Junior' can make even the toughest conditions look like a stroll.

**Viv Richards. He had a few mannerisms that intimidated bowlers.
One was his right hand coming off the bat at the end of the shot — it
was the sign of the long bat follow-through, a sure sign the ball
had been hit a mile.**

A full house in and on centre stage the irrepressible **Mr. Ian Botham**. 'Beefy' was a champion all rounder who could do just about anything. He once scored a Test double-century against India at the rate of 92 runs per 100 balls. And, he once snatched away from Australia an 'unloseable' Ashes Test.

ABOVE & OPPOSITE:
Guts and grace, Steve Waugh and David Gower. I've made
Steve the captain of my World XII. We all loved David Gower
for the easy way he hit his shots.

**Matthew Elliott. Some people might be surprised to see a player
of such inexperience in my World XII but he's got all the qualities
of a champion. I predict he'll make 5,000 Test runs.**

Ian Healy. Best wicketkeeper in the world by a long way.

One of the great things about English cricket — apart from its history — is that its followers see Test cricket as the ultimate form of the game. That is why Australian and world cricket need England to be successful. It keeps that link with history strong and keeps Test cricket healthy. That doesn't mean England should live in the past, but that the past should be part of the future. We've modernised the game in Australia over the past 10 years while still making sure Test cricket is number one and that the Shield continues to produce Test players.

English cricket is important to me for a number of reasons, mostly because it was in England in 1993 that I really established my international career. I'd struggled early, then improved in the series against the West Indies in 1992–3, continued that improvement in New Zealand and then took good form to England in 1993. It was that Ashes series that set me up. Like every Australian cricketer I've wondered what it would be like to play a season of county cricket, and maybe at some stage in the future I'll be able to find out. It would be a great challenge to take up after my Test career is over and one I'll look at when that times comes. Maybe earlier.

As for 1997, I can say here that I started that Ashes tour with a personal goal. I don't talk about those sorts of goals in public, but I can say here that my aim in England in 1997 was to take more wickets than I did in 1993. I took 34 then so my aim in 1997 was to take at least 35 — that's six a Test which is a very high strike-rate, but I wanted to prove to myself and to everyone else that I had recovered fully from my finger operation and had finally got back to a situation where I was improving again. To beat my 1993 wicket tally was the best way to add a personal element to my motivation. Being motivated for the team was easy because, after all, it was Australia versus England, another Ashes series and Australians love nothing more than beating the Poms at their own game.

But I must finish by saying that this has been written before the 1997 Ashes series. Hopefully I won't end up with egg on my face.

Let's hope England have improved. Let the summer begin. Hopefully, it's a great series.

Captain Warne

When I was appointed Victorian captain a few months after the end of the 1995–6 season, people wondered why I was given the job if I was going to be away with the Australian team so often. It's a fair enough question but a captain's job doesn't end when he walks off the field. The captain goes out to toss, uses his imagination and experience to set fields and use his bowlers, but he also has to mould a happy and ambitious team. Most of that work is done outside the picket fence. Team spirit is important when tough situations occur on the field, when teamwork and determination will often see you through.

I had not really thought about becoming Victorian captain until the previous season, 1994–5, when all the trouble with Les Stillman and Dean Jones began to upset the players. I began to think then that I might be able to make a difference, to bring the team back together if I was given the captaincy. I had been captain of a lot of junior teams as a kid, representative teams which were full of good players. Along the way more than a few people thought I had leadership qualities. I thought the experience I'd gathered at junior level would help me as a captain at first-class level, although I was still apprehensive about taking over Victoria in the months leading up to the season. As a player rather than a leader during the Jones-Stillman years I spoke to my teammates a lot and knew why they were upset. I also had a fair idea of how to get them back to playing well as a united team. Knowing that John Scholes would be coach also gave me confidence. He is a little on the conservative side, from the old school, and I am a little on the other side so I thought we'd make a good pair. Plus we enjoy each other's company. We're mates as well as colleagues.

On or off the field, one of the most important jobs for the captain of a cricket team is to get the best out of his players. I see my role as captain as getting the best out of every individual player in the state squad. To do that I have to know what makes each individual tick. I suppose it was

STEVE CUFF/SPORTSEXPOSURE

**Always in the eye. It's my captaincy debut for Victoria,
a tough game against NSW at the SCG, and the pressure
is still on, even though I'm off the field.**

because I was recovering from my finger operation that I had plenty of time
to spend with the squad during my first pre-season as captain, and I'm sure
that helped me settle into the new job and helped the players get used to a
new set-up. Once you know each individual you know how to get to them,
when to ride them hard, when to ease off, when to give them a rocket, when
not. Every player is different and a captain cannot treat them all the same.
I suppose that was one thing I did not like about the Academy when I was
there — the tendency to treat everyone the same. It does not work. We
don't want robots playing the game. Characters have always added to the
great game and they should be allowed room to be themselves. Take Merv
Hughes, for example. He is a fantastic and loyal friend and we all love him.
Why? Because he is a character.

   During the Super 8s tournament before the 1996–7 season I asked Ian
Chappell, one of Australia's greatest captains and a good friend, to speak to
the Victorian squad. Ian agreed and what he said went to the core of this
idea of a captain knowing his players. Although he was not talking about
captains but about all players, he said that as a player you have to know
yourself and your game well. You have to know what you need to do to
perform the next day — whether you go out and have a few beers, go to

bed early, go out for a quiet meal. You have to know what makes you play at your best. And that applies to the captain even more than other players, because the captain has to know not only himself but everyone else as well.

If a good captain has to be a good judge of character I reckon i've got a chance of doing a decent job as Victorian captain. If I'm good at anything I reckon I'm not too bad at judging people. Usually I can judge someone's personality pretty quickly. I can meet a bloke and get him talking for 20 minutes and generally I'll know what he is like. I think I inherited that ability from my mother Brigitte who is a very shrewd judge of people. I can introduce her to someone, give her 15 minutes to get to know them, then ask her what she thinks about them. She'll be spot on nine times out of ten.

Something I've always enjoyed doing in the dressingroom is observing how different players react to different situations and that is something that a captain can use in motivating his players. Once you get to know players you can generally tell if someone is on song or not. And you can tell how the team as a whole is feeling by the atmosphere in the dressingroom. If we won the toss and were batting I used to enjoy watching Craig McDermott. It was quite funny because he would be very lively, jumping all around the room, no doubt pleased that he could relax for a day or so while the batsmen did their job. If we were bowling Craig would be much quieter and more serious, trying to focus on how he was going to bowl. Glenn McGrath is fairly subdued before play, and is always one of the last to get ready. He has taken over the Merv Hughes role as the team pest, throwing things at people, especially Mark Waugh, and annoying us any way he can. You need those sorts of people in a team to ease the tension. For the past year or so, Glenn has been bowling very well and so has been full of confidence. He's known he's going to go out there and bowl well. Andrew Bichel is another good bloke to have around. He is a livewire and a real fighter and so he's a good influence in the rooms. Paul Reiffel is pretty relaxed and takes it fairly easy before a day's play. But looks can deceive with 'Pistol'. He is a determined cricketer and can focus on the day ahead very well. David Boon was also pretty quiet, but when he spoke we all paid attention because we had so much respect for his achievements in the game and for the sort of person he is. If we were batting Boonie would be quiet, sitting in his spot in the rooms waiting to go out to bat, building his concentration, with a couple of bits of chewing gum next to his helmet while having a quiet smoke. I was always impressed with the way Boonie prepared in the nets of a morning — actually any time he had a hit in the nets. He always played as if he were batting in a Test match. He very rarely played rash shots and was always committed. Perhaps he learnt that from AB, who also never wasted a net. I always enjoyed bowling to AB and Boonie in the nets because it made me work hard.

Before a day's play Steve Waugh does plenty of encouraging. Steve also reminds us if we're bowling to put on our baggy green caps because now we always wear them for the first session. It was a great idea of Steve's but Mark Waugh, though he likes the idea, still prefers his white floppy hat. It can be fairly tense before the start of a Test, especially before the captain goes out to toss. Once we know whether we're batting or bowling everyone relaxes a little, as we know what we have to do for the day. Soon after that you find everyone goes into their shell a little as they start focusing on their particular role for the day. I try to get myself going by encouraging the other guys — the fast bowlers if we're in the field, the openers if we're batting. That also gets me going because I know a Test is about to start and soon we'll either be out there trying to take wickets or sitting in the viewing room watching closely as the openers face the new ball. It's a very tense time, the first session of a Test match. If we are bowling Mark Waugh tells us to save all the encouragement for the field. He reckons there is no need to get too worked up in the dressingroom, that it is better to save it for the middle. That just shows how individuals prepare in their own way. There's no right and wrong in this and it is best for a team if everyone has the chance to prepare in the way that best suits them.

If I spot someone who is perhaps short of form or nervous for some reason I'll usually go over and have a word. "Come on, we're all with you. Be positive. Good luck." It's nothing original or startling but even if you've played 100 Test matches you still appreciate a pat on the bum and a few words of support. Generally a captain can tell if someone is worried. Every player likes to feel that the captain thinks something of him, thinks that he deserves some personal encouragement. It doesn't have to be much, just a few words when a guy is down.

On the field, a good captain will know when to speak to a bowler and when to leave him alone. With relatively inexperienced players, the captain might be wise to take time to help the bowler set his fields and plan a strategy. The skipper will also be aware of the rhythm of the play and will be prepared to break that rhythm if he thinks it will suit his team or a particular player. All good captains know these things and will alter the rhythm of the game to suit his players' needs. A captain who fields at first slip, like Mark Taylor, can either tell the mid-off fieldsman to chat to the bowler or he can slow the game right down by coming up from slip for a

chat. That can break the pattern of the game or the rhythm of the batsman. These are some of the little things that make a good captain and make
the job interesting.

I like to think that I would always be a risk-taker on the field, a captain
prepared to take a gamble and try something rather than let the game drift
while I wait for inspiration. The best captains are those who have the courage to trust their gut feelings and act on them before the moment slips away.
Of course not all people have the right gut feelings. But there is only one
way to find out about yours if you're the skipper and that is to try them
out in play. I remember a game in South Africa in 1994 when AB suddenly
moved to midwicket and soon after he took a catch there. Later when I
asked AB why he did that he said he didn't really know, he just had a gut
feeling about it. He told me that if ever I became a captain I should always

RAY TITUS/NEWS LTD

**Mark Taylor enjoys the moment of winning back the Frank
Worrell Trophy. Mark is a lucky captain. Cricket 'luck' is a strange
thing ... I reckon it comes from confidence in your ability.**

trust in my gut feelings and act on them immediately. Don't ever hesitate. It was good advice.

Captains also need luck and I'd say that Mark Taylor is a lucky captain. And a very good one as well. He tries a lot of moves and most of the time they succeed. Other captains might try similar things but they would not work. So what reason do you give for the difference? Sometimes you make a move but your bowler is not good enough to carry it through for you. There have never been many great captains of poor teams. How would you know whether someone is a clever captain if every time he tries something his players let him down? You have to pick the right bowler for that tactic and that moment, but you also need players good enough to support those decisions. On top of that you still need some luck. And in cricket luck is a strange thing.

I reckon luck often comes from believing in yourself and trusting yourself in tough situations. Many people have luck in cricket and many more don't. And some are just kissed on the ....! Merv Hughes was a great fast bowler, a legend, and he had that luck. When Merv was bowling and Australia needed a wicket, he would get that wicket every time. As well as luck he had great determination and the Phar Lap heart. I think I have that sort of luck when I play. When you're confident and you think things are going really well you usually make your own luck. If you're not quite sure about something, or you don't feel fully comfortable with what you are doing, that is when you don't enjoy much luck. It is amazing what confidence can do. If you're confident you can do anything whether it's in sport, business, television, politics or whatever. Mark Taylor is like that and that is why the things he tries almost always come off. He is confident about what he is doing, he knows it is the right thing to do and it works. And that is great for the Australian cricket team. In my early days as captain of Victoria I think I had similar luck. Touch wood it continues.

In my first Sheffield Shield game as Victorian captain we played New South Wales at the SCG. They were cruising at about 3/150 when I decided to try something unexpected. Shane Lee was going well and was the wicket we needed. He likes to hit the ball hard so I decided it was worth trying to tempt him by bowling our opening batsman, Matthew Elliott. I'd been encouraging all our batsmen to bowl some sort of spin and Matty's left-armers showed promise in the nets, although I don't think he really expected to get a bowl. The on-side boundary was close so the temptation for Shane was pretty high. I knew Shane from the World Cup and I knew he would not want to let Matty get away with a few overs. He'd want to assert himself and belt Matty out of the park, but at the same time he would be scared stiff of getting out to him. If as a captain you can get a batsman thinking in contradictory ways you stand a very good chance of forcing an error. I told Matty I would give him two or three overs and that he should toss the ball in the air. I told him I didn't care whether he got hit for a couple of sixes. I wanted him to get a wicket. I set a fairly attacking field to tempt Shane to slog one over the top. If he did that a few times, I was going to adjust the field and force him to try to hit somewhere else.

Matty was keen to have a go and it was not long before I could see that Shane was desperate to go after him. In the end Shane ran down the wicket at him, went for a big hit and was stumped beautifully by Darren Berry. I gave Matty one more over then took him off. Like a typical bowler, he wasn't happy. In that situation I was lucky but there was a plan behind the luck. Basically the way I play my cricket is that I take a risk, hopefully a calculated risk. When you try something like that it does not always work but even when it doesn't it can make the batsman wary the next time you're doing something different. I remember bowling to Jamie Cox six years ago in Tasmania. It was the last ball before lunch and I told our captain Simon O'Donnell that I was going to bowl my Derryn Hinch ball.

"What do you mean?" Simon asked.

"Expect the unexpected," I said. "Move the man at square leg a bit closer and watch what happens."

Then I bowled a huge pie floater, a slow high full toss, at Jamie's head and he hit it just short of the man at square leg. It was not out but it was close. I tried it again in a Shield game this season, but I'd forgotten the new rule that makes a head high full toss a no-ball. I out-smarted myself on that one.

Another off-field area where a captain can be important is in relations with officials. To my mind the captain represents his players in their dealings with officials and if the crunch comes he has to back his players. If something affecting the Victorian team is happening and we don't like it I will stand up for the players. If I cop a fine or reprimand from the VCA, so be it. I would rather stand up and make sure the players are being looked after than stay on side with the administrators. Ideally the administrators should feel part of the whole side. We should all be going in the same direction. One unit. If a captain loses the respect of his players he's gone as a leader. I know from talking to past players that Ian Chappell was a strong players' man and that's why he always had their loyalty.

I suppose one area that I might find difficult as a captain is deciding

THE FAIRFAX PHOTO LIBRARY

**Watching AB's mind at work in my first Test
against India at the SCG in 1992.**

when to bowl myself or when to take myself off. Like all bowlers, I love to have that ball in my hand and to be in the contest, but as a captain I also have to know when it's time to give someone else a go. The other side of the coin is that I mightn't bowl myself enough. That's when you need to keep a cool head and a little distance from the action so your thinking is clear. It also helps to have experienced senior players out there with you whose advice you trust. Although that situation could cause problems for a bowler-captain, I'm sure it can be offset by the fact that a bowler-captain understands his other bowlers better than a batsman-captain. Bowlers should understand field placements and tactics better than batsmen and that should be an advantage for any bowler who becomes a skipper.

I've been happy with my first season as captain of Victoria although the players would be the best people to ask. I've certainly been prepared to try a few things and to be aggressive. I've also tried to make the VCA and Victorian public go in one direction and get behind the Bushrangers. The two captains I've played under for Australia have been outstanding in differing ways and I would like to combine elements of both in my captaincy career. AB led mainly by example. Tubby has taken more risks but he's had a strong team to back him. When you're winning more often than not the captain can afford to be aggressive. When you're not winning too often, as it was for AB in his early years as captain, you tend to err on the conservative side.

One of the major differences between AB and Tubby as captains is that Tubby talks much more. He runs all the team meetings and is always chatting to his players. If he thinks you have a problem he'll pull you aside for a chat about it. He tries to clear up everything and make sure everyone knows what they are doing and where they are going. In general, AB never talked one on one that much with the players. He kept things short and sharp and got on with the game. If you sat at a bar and had a beer with AB you would get to know him and see what a great bloke he was. Over a few beers at a bar in a hotel somewhere you could learn a lot from AB. For us younger players starting out in the early 1990s there could not have been a better man to learn from than Allan Border. I learnt a heap off him. He occasionally gave me a hard time, but it was always for my own good. We are still very close and he will be one of my close friends forever.

On the field AB would come up with some ideas and see what I thought about my bowling, but usually in the end he would let me set my own fields and work out my own tactics; whereas Tubby will ask me to think about my field but if he does not like something he will say so and then go ahead and do it his way.

SHAUN BOTTERILL/ALL SPORT

Captain of Australia ... it's a nice thought. If I was offered the job it would be impossible to refuse, but gee ... when I see the pressures Allan Border and Mark Taylor have had to endure life just as a player seems very attractive.

AB's record as captain is fantastic and there in the record books for all to see. Tubby is doing all the right things at the moment. He never lets a game drift and he does some things out of left field which make life interesting in the middle. He always tries to make the game happen which is a great approach. I think Mark Taylor is a very good captain, just as Allan Border was for so many years. Hopefully Mark continues that way.

I suppose I am a mix of all the captains I've had together with a few of my own ideas. Since I became Victorian captain people have started speculating about whether I am on my way to the Australian job. I suppose I am a chance, although a lot will depend on how I'm going at the time. I think most of the senior players will retire around the same time. I'd love to keep playing for Victoria for a few years after retiring from international cricket, but the time will come when the pressures of playing for Australia will become overpowering.

So who knows what will happen? Three years is a long time in cricket and I will never get ahead of myself. I might be offered the Australian captaincy and it would be impossible to refuse such an honour, but sometimes

I think about the pressures Allan Border and Mark Taylor have endured and I wonder whether I would want all those extra burdens. I cannot believe Mike Atherton has lasted so long while England has been losing so often. He can't be enjoying it. By the end of the tour to South Africa in April 1997 I was so tired I said I wondered whether the Ashes tour that year would be my last and I felt I had enough on my plate without the Australian captaincy. Because of all the pressures connected with my bowling and my high profile I sometimes think I'd be better off to remain just a player. Maybe a good deputy. Also, you have to make sure you are playing well if you are to become captain. Mark Taylor has been under enormous pressure recently because he has not been making runs. He was probably lucky that we won the Test series against South Africa. But as I'm writing this we're off to the UK and hopefully Tub will make a bucket full of runs on that tour.

Of course, if I was the best candidate for the job and the selectors and the ACB wanted me to do it I would not refuse. How could I? But I doubt I will be offered it anyway. If Steve Waugh, Ian Healy and Mark Taylor play for another three years I will be 30. If I became captain at 30 I'd probably only be in the job for a couple of years. Even at 31 I might have had enough of life on the road and all the pressures associated with the game. I might also have a couple of children by then and want to spend more time with them. It's hard to know how I will feel in a few years time. Anything can happen and it's wise not to get too far ahead of yourself. My finger might play up again; my shoulder might give up the ghost; I might just lose form and my place in the team. I could also find the best form of my life. It's all hypothetical at this stage. If my form was very good, I would probably feel like playing on for another five or six years and the captaincy would certainly add a new dimension to my cricket career. Who knows?

Family Favourites

Every cricketer and every cricket fan would love to be a selector. Every player has an opinion on his teammates and opponents and most conversations in loungerooms and pubs end up being about selection. So I could not resist choosing a few teams myself.

The first two teams come from my backyard games with my brother Jason. We had a long list of our favourite players from Australia and the world. They might not have been the very best at the time — although a glance at the teams I've chosen suggests they were all high class — but they certainly had character. Our favourites were players who were entertainers, good to watch with qualities that made them stand out. That's what we liked about them: they all had something distinctive we could imitate and mimicry was very much part of our games. I was born in 1969 so I was only young when many of these players began their careers. But I remember them either from footage or from seeing them live on television. As well, some played in World Series Cricket in the late 1970s and the emphasis there was on talent and entertainment. That was the way I liked my cricket back then and basically the way I still like it.

So, my Australian and World backyard teams are:

MY BACKYARD AUSTRALIAN XII

1 — Rick McCosker
A solid, reliable opener. I, like many people, will never forget McCosker coming out to bat with his broken jaw wrapped in bandages in Australia's second innings of the Centenary Test. He made important runs too. Heroic stuff. In our backyard games he was hit on the jaw quite a few times.

2 — Bruce Laird
Pure guts. Laird was a hero because of his no-nonsense technique and great

courage against West Indian pace. He took plenty on the body in our backyard but never took a backward step.

3 — Ian Chappell (c)

He had everything. A great captain, a great attacking batsman and no end of mannerisms ripe for imitating. We loved the ritual of Chappell adjusting his pads, his cap, and especially his protector before each ball. And the way he wore his collar up and scratched out his centre on the crease in that assertive way. After that would come another bouncer and another ferocious hook shot.

4 — Greg Chappell

A great batsman with a near perfect technique. He had an upright, supremely confident stride to the pitch which Jason and I enjoyed imitating. It was always a delight to play the G Chappell on-drive.

5 — Allan Border

As much guts as Laird but even more ability. Little did we know that AB would go on past 11,000 Test runs and 150 Tests. Or that I would one day have the pleasure of actually playing in the same Australian team.

6 — Doug Walters

A compulsory selection in any all-time backyard team. The ultimate attacking player who could break all the rules of technique and still hit it for 4. His hook shot off Bob Willis for 6 off the last ball of the day to give Dougie a hundred in a session in Perth was legendary. As kids we watched it on video a few years later and loved it.

7 — Rod Marsh

Another legend. Tough as nails and, although built like a rugby player, an athletic 'keeper to the great Dennis Lillee.

8 — Richie Benaud

Although I didn't see much of Richie bowl I have become interested in his career, like he has in mine. He is always spot on in his commentary and was obviously a great player. He wore his collar up and the buttons on his shirt undone. He had style.

9 — Max Walker

One of cricket's more awkward bowling actions gave us plenty of material to take the mickey out of Victoria's favourite son. He was also a very fine swing and seam bowler.

10 — Dennis Lillee

The greatest bowler of his era and one of the very best of all time. We pre-ferred him in his long-haired, tearaway days when his appeal was as aggres-sive as any ever seen. A great character and a great champion.

11 — Jeff Thomson

Lillee's mate had a great action — unique and spectacular. That front leg lifted so high before the right arm came thumping down. In our games, Thommo had a licence to bowl as fast and as short as he wanted.

12 — Gary Gilmour

Big Gus was also a favourite, although this was because he reminded us of those talented kids who are just not motivated enough to make the most of their talent. When he was on song, Gilmour could swing the ball all over the place and his hitting in the lower order was sensational. He would have been a very good one-day player too. Twelfth man more for his dressingroom presence than his all-round fielding.

MY BACKYARD WORLD XII

1 — Gordon Greenidge

The classical, brooding opener with just about the best technique in the game. We loved his signature swivel-pull off his hips when the front leg would lift flamboy-antly as the ball sped towards or over square leg.

2 — Desmond Haynes

No Greenidge without Haynes. They were the best opening pair in the game with heaps of flair and confidence.

VIV JENKINS/AUSTRALIAN CRICKET BOARD

Gordon Greenidge. Just about the best technique in the game.

3 — David Gower

The best-looking left-hander in the game. We loved Gower's casual walk to the crease and the easy way he hit his shots.

4 — Viv Richards

'The Man'. At his peak the best batsman in the world with the swaggering walk to match. Viv had plenty of mannerisms, especially the way he chewed his gum, and every one was designed to make the bowlers think they were in for another hiding.

5 — Derek Randall

The Pommy fidget who played that memorable innings in the Centenary Test in Melbourne in 1977. I'm told he was as mad as a cut snake but he played one great innings, against Lillee too. His loose, wobbly body was perfect for imitating.

6 — Ian Botham

England's version of 'The Man'. A great allrounder who only ever attacked. He could bat, bowl and catch and he had tremendous star quality. His ability to change the game was second to none. Every kid wanted to bat like Viv or Dougie and win Test matches on his own like 'Beefy'.

7 — Jeff Dujon

Cool, calm and always collected, Dujon was spectacular when he dived or leapt to take an edge off one of the West Indian quicks. And he was forever making runs at number 7 just when all the top batsmen were gone. He always performed under pressure.

8 — Malcolm Marshall

Probably as good as Lillee and very, very fast. His sliding action was different and gave us good material for the backyard impersonations. At express pace Marshall could swing the ball or bounce it up under your nose. AB said he was the hardest bowler he ever faced. Another legend of West Indian cricket.

9 — Abdul Qadir

The great spinner of the era and a leg-spinner as well. Qadir's twirling fingers and swirling arms seemed to mesmerise batsmen. It was action that was a delight to impersonate.

10 — Joel Garner

'Big Bird' was just so huge. To kids he was a giant. He looked as if he lumbered to the crease and just rolled his arms over but he was actually fast, had nasty bounce and was the most accurate bowler of the time. An awesome sight.

Abdul Qadir. Cast a spell over batsmen with his swirling, twirling arms!

11 — Garth Le Roux

We liked him because he was big, blond and fast. He was a little like Thommo in that he just ran in and let it go as fast as he could. It was the perfect approach as far as we were concerned.

12 — Gus Logie

At his best a great fielder, either in the covers or short-leg. Very speedy across the turf, Logie was the 1980s equivalent of Jonty Rhodes.

While I am in selector mode it is hard to resist the chance to pick the best Test and one-day teams from the cricketers playing at present. Anyone who reckons the game is not as good as it was should imagine the challenges presented by a few games against these teams.

MY CURRENT TEST WORLD XII

1 — Sachin Tendulkar

A class batsman, with an excellent technique and plenty of power. For balance he would have to open but he is easily good enough to do it. Why not get him in early? I haven't seen anyone hit the ball harder.

2 — Matthew Elliott

Every team needs a player picked as much for potential as runs on the board. Soon enough, Matty Elliott will have those runs. He has a simple, correct technique, time to see the ball and play his shots and an appetite for big hundreds. He'll make at least 5000 Test runs for Australia. Fingers crossed.

3 — Brian Lara

At his best Lara is just about impossible to control. He has all the shots, can invent others and loves to be centre stage.

4 — Mark Waugh

His century against South Africa in the Second Test in Port Elizabeth in March 1997 not only won Australia the match and the series, but it proved that Mark can make even the toughest conditions look like a stroll. Even in this company he is outstanding in the field, but he needs to work on his off-spinners.

5 — Steve Waugh (c)

His is the most valuable wicket in the world at present, partly because it is the hardest to take. Mentally tough, vastly experienced, Steve should be captain of this World team. England players should take note of 'Tugga'.

6 — Brian McMillan

The best allrounder in the game and such a good bloke to play against, he must be great to play with. He adds a sense of humour to a highly competitive attitude and plenty of natural talent.

7 — Ian Healy

The best wicketkeeper in the world by a long way. Has made three Test centuries to prove his value with the bat. An outstanding cricketer, and a great team man.

8 — Wasim Akram (vc)

A true great, Wasim can be almost unplayable when he gets that reverse swing going. A tremendous hitter and a very good captain. I'd make him Steve Waugh's deputy.

9 — Shane Warne

I reserve the right to give myself a game with these blokes. How could I resist?

10 — Curtly Ambrose

A fantastic bowler, the best and most consistent paceman of his era.

11 — Glenn McGrath

Has shown over the past two years that he is one of the very best fast bowlers in the game. Can reverse swing and bowl well in all conditions.

12 — Jonty Rhodes

The best fielder of his era, a cheery and energetic bloke. The perfect 12th man.

Wasim Akram. I'd make him Steve Waugh's vice-captain in my World team.

VIV JENKINS/AUSTRALIAN CRICKET BOARD

MY CURRENT ONE-DAY WORLD XII

1 — Sachin Tendulkar

Saeed Anwar is unlucky to miss out, but how can I go past Tendulkar and M Waugh as one-day openers?

2 — Mark Waugh

One of the best one-day batsmen of all time. Brilliant anywhere in the field.

3 — Brian Lara

When he goes off in a one-dayer he stands at the crease and hits boundaries to all corners of the ground.

4 — Hansie Cronje

An excellent one-day batsman capable of hitting bowlers out of the ground and the attack. A very useful medium-pacer with a knack for taking important wickets.

5 — Steve Waugh (c)
Coolest in a crisis and the most experienced one-day cricketer in the world.

6 — Michael Bevan
The best middle order one-day bat in world cricket, who can cleverly control the pace of an innings. Brilliant in the field and a dangerous spin bowler.

7 — Ian Healy
Superb with the gloves and inventive with the bat.

8 — Wasim Akram (vc)
Explosive with ball and bat. Remember that over in the World Cup final against England in Melbourne in 1992?

9 — Shane Warne
No comment.

10 — Curtly Ambrose
Too tall, too accurate. One of the best one-day bowlers of all time.

11 — Glenn McGrath
His ability to maintain good pace with great control makes him a terrific one-day bowler.

12 — Jonty Rhodes
Simply the best fielder in the game and, in one-day matches, often worth a couple of run-outs.

No doubt my choices would start a few arguments, but that is what selecting is about, isn't it? These are my favourite players, the ones I'd most like to pay to watch or to play with. And although I believe that Test and one-day teams will differ more and more over the next few years, most of the names in one list are to be found in the other. When you are talking about the very best players in the world, that is no surprise. They are good enough to adapt their skills to either game.

Smile on the face of the tiger! Glenn McGrath gets into my world's best simply because he's just that — one of the world's great fast bowlers.

The Future

Since I started my international career in the season of 1991–2, the game of cricket has progressed and grown around the world. There seems to be more cricket played, more money being generated by the game, more television coverage and more ideas about where cricket is going in the next 10 years. Overall, that situation is healthy, although the game still has to choose the best way forward.

I agree with two recent suggestions about changes in the game. Firstly a system to rate the Test teams in a World Championship table is a great idea that would help the marketing of Test cricket. More and more Test matches are ending in results than was the case a decade ago. Australia's three Tests against South Africa in March 1997 ended in three results and the games had everything you'd want — a dominant performance by Australia in the First, a tense, close contest dominated by bowlers in the Second and a comeback by South Africa in the Third. The action was high class and the players strongly committed.

The foundation is there for the administrators at the International Cricket Council to build on the return of Test cricket. It is the most important game for the players and if a World Test Championship system of some sort can be developed it will add another dimension to the game. Australia, England and the West Indies all like to play plenty of Test series but the other countries have moved away from Tests to the one-day game, mainly for the larger revenue. I know that players like India's captain Sachin Tendulkar and leg-spinner Anil Kumble want to play more Test cricket. During my career Australia has played about two one-day games to a Test. The subcontinent countries have been playing three one-dayers to each Test. That imbalance between the programs followed by countries on the subcontinent and the others needs to be fixed. The prestige of a World Championship for Test cricket will help rearrange programming. Sri Lanka won the last World Cup and can call themselves World Champions, although that title comes from success at only one form of the game. If there were a title for Test cricket as well, the standings of each country in each game would be there for all to see. I think in Test cricket we would be Number 1, the Windies 2, Pakistan 3, South Africa 4, India 5, England 6, New Zealand 7, Sri Lanka 8 and Zimbabwe 9.

The second good idea to have come out in recent times is that of playing a World Cup every two years instead of four. Four years is a long time between tournaments and team personnel can change dramatically over that period. After all, Australia is on a two-yearly Test cycle with England and the West Indies. Play them at home and two years later play them away. That is basically how it works and such a programming system gives some continuity to the cricket. Teams will still change but not completely as can happen over four years. As well, a two-yearly World Cup would be a marketing boon and would also slow up the growth of all these one-off one-day tournaments that bob up anywhere anytime these days. Countries would have to organise their one-day tournaments with an eye on preparations for the next World Cup. Cricket could concentrate on those major two-yearly tournaments. As long as Test cricket is promoted via a points table for a World Test title, more World Cups should not damage the position of Test cricket.

The return of spin bowling has increased run rates in Tests, but they could improve further. The only way to stop teams bowling their overs too slowly is to fine them in runs not money. A number of runs, maybe 20 for each over not bowled in time, should come off the team's first innings total. The ICC referees now think that suspending players for poor behaviour works better than fining. Why not apply that theory to slow over rates?

With so much one-day cricket being played all year round all over the cricket world, some of the games can be predictable, even dead when one team chases a small target. I'm sure we'll see more music, songs and entertainment at one-day matches, even coloured hats. They will become more like baseball games in the US. The rules will have to follow to some extent. As those rules always favour the batsmen why not add to the batting spectacle by increasing the value for boundaries? On some of our big grounds in Australia ropes could bring the boundaries closer and a 4 could be worth 6 and a 6 maybe 8. Also, if the bowlers bowl a wide or a no-ball, the batter could receive a free hit off the next ball. The only way he can get out would be to run himself out. Imagine the expectation in the crowd. To stop games becoming predictable, we could have a rule that allows the batsmen a five-over period in which the fielding restrictions for the first 15 overs apply again — only two men outside the circle. It would be up to the batting captain to designate when the five overs will start. When does he do it? Which bowlers does he use? I know captains have plenty on their plates in one-day cricket and that this would add another tricky problem, but it would spark up the tactics and the action.

Although the Test and one-day teams chosen in the last chapter contained many of the same players, I do think that there will be more and more team changes from one game to the other. One-day cricket is getting faster and tougher physically, partly because players are improving their skills but also because there is so much of it. If one-day cricket is about entertainment even more than Test cricket, then it makes sense to keep bringing young players through to the one-day team. If an older player is better then he should play. But the younger guys will play an adventurous game and the older players can concentrate on Test cricket where they will last longer. Obviously player payments need to take account of this and that is something the Australian Cricketers' Association will discuss with the ACB.

The situation for Australia in South Africa on both tours worked well because the one-day series were held after the Test series. Even though eight games was too many, they had the right idea. In Australia we move between the two forms of the game and it can confuse supporters and affect players' form. Most of the players are used to it but it is definitely easier to finish a Test series then switch fully to one-day thinking, or vice versa. Most players would like to see improvement in the programming. For some, far fewer one-day games and more Tests; for others fewer one-day series. Hopefully administrators will listen to the players and sort out the programming on a worldwide basis. If so, it should be possible to arrange it so that Test and one-day series were played in one hit and at different times of a tour. South Africa was perfect for Australia because in 1997 we were able to rest injured or tired players after the Test series and replace them for the one-day games with fresh and mostly younger players, two of whom made their one-day international debuts. No Test player wants to miss out on the one-day team. It is a matter of pride in his ability that makes a player want to be seen as being good enough for both forms of the game. But as players start to suffer from the amount of cricket they will need more rests. The whole system will have to be more flexible.

I think the best two umpires at the moment are David Shepherd (UK) and Steve Bucknor (West Indies), but generally the standard of umpiring seems to have dropped in the past few years and the game needs to attract more ex-first class and Test players into umpiring. That will mean better

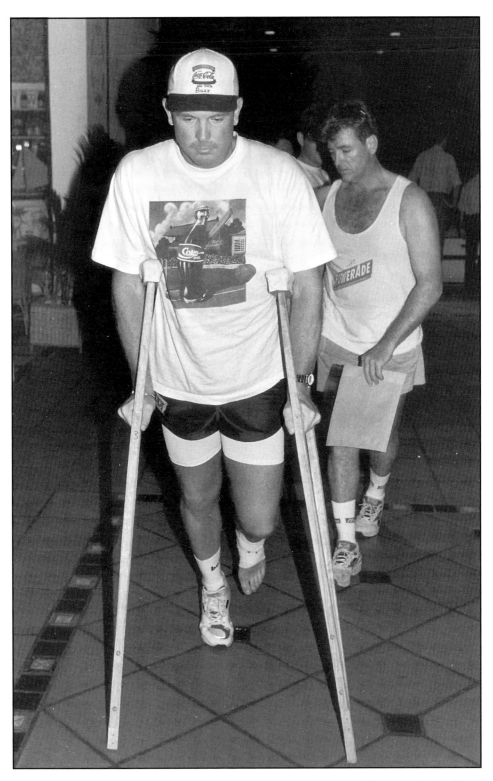

The end of the road for Craig McDermott. At his shoulder Errol Alcott, the man whose ever-tougher task it is to try to keep us on the field and injury-free. Our cricket workload has increased dramatically.

pay as an incentive for players to stay in the game as umpires and that extra investment in the game would definitely improve the standard of play.
Another way to improve umpiring could be to try using three umpires a
Test. Each umpire would sit out a session at a time and they would rotate
through a five-day Test match. We once used that system in Shield cricket
in Australia and I think it would help the umpires cope with the extra work
and pressures they have these days. They could rotate from the third umpire on the video to out in the middle. I don't think that the umpires should
receive any more help from the video umpire system. The video replays are
fine for the line decisions they are used for now, but for judging catches
they can be deceptive. In most cases, the umpires in the middle are in a
better position to judge a catch than their mate off the field in the TV room.

Although technology might not be able to go much further in umpiring, it looks like being a growth area in coaching. First came Spin Cam
and now the South Africans are working on a system of virtual reality where
a batsman will put on a headset and feel like he is facing a bowler — in full
3-D. Spin Cam was a very good innovation. It was first seen in Australia
during our successful tour to the West Indies in 1995. I'm sure it added to
people's enjoyment and knowledge and to the tools available for coaching.
It might even have helped a few batsmen have more of an understanding
of what I was up to, but then my explanations on some of the footage might
not have been entirely accurate. And the old saying is right: even if the
batsman picks it, he still has to play it. And in a split second. As well, a
batsman cannot predict what a bowler is going to do next and technology
will not tell him. Each ball spins and bounces differently and the batsman
has to cope each time. Virtual reality might be even better than Spin Cam,
but there is nothing better than being there in the flesh, up close. The best
way to learn about a new bowler is to face him. The next best way is to put
on a hat and a pair of sunglasses and wander up to the back of the nets and
have a look for yourself.

Since the Australian team came back from the tour to Pakistan in 1994,
we have set up the Australian Cricketers' Association. England has had one
for years but not Australia. We have set ours up strongly and have experienced businessmen as advisers. The hope is that there will also be an international association to represent the interests of all international cricketers.
That way the players will have a say in programming, tour itineraries and
rule changes. The more players can concentrate on cricket the better — as
long as their Players' Association is keeping them up to date on off-the-
field matters.

As I've said before I'm not into statistics too much. Some cricketers are, although we do know where we stand roughly on the main things like average and aggregate. One statistic that I know of is that I have a chance of becoming the first Australian player to take 300 wickets and score 1000 runs in Test cricket. I'm not far short of the runs, and I could even make the 300 wickets some time during the next Australian summer. I'd be proud of that achievement. It's one I definitely have my eyes on. People ask me how keen I am on being the first player to take 500 Test wickets. Frankly it seems a long way off at the moment. All I want to do is keep playing for as long as I am enjoying it. I don't really know when that enjoyment will end. When it does, I will retire and then I'll know how many Test wickets I will have taken. So many things can go wrong in your career that there is no point getting ahead of yourself. Wicket by wicket, game by game, day by day, series by series — whichever way you want to say it, it is best to take things one at a time. If my body and my mind can keep going for long enough then I'd be delighted to take 500 Test wickets, but who knows what will happen. The main thing is that I remain a member of a successful Australian team. Since I started playing, we've established ourselves as the best Test team in the world and still one of the best one-day teams. I want to be a part of an Australian team that can claim both titles. In Tests we've beaten the West Indies in the past two series — away and at home — and before this 1997 Ashes tour we'd won the past four series against England. We've beaten every country in a series somewhere. We came second in the 1996 World Cup and I'd love to play in an Australian team that won the World Cup.

After cricket, there will be more cricket, I suppose. After I've finished international cricket I want to play on for a couple of seasons with Victoria before trying my hand at something off the field. Some coaching, some involvement with Victorian cricket, a few business interests, maybe some television commentary. I don't know what the mix will be and at this stage I don't need to know — as long as I keep taking wickets for Australia.

Scoreboard

As at May 1, 1997

TEST CRICKET

Debut: 1991-92 Australia v India, Sydney

BOWLING RECORD AGAINST EACH COUNTRY

Country	Debut	M	Balls	Mdns	Runs	Wkts	Avrge	5	10	Best	Stk/Rt
India	1991-92	2	408	9	228	1	228.00	-	-	1/150	408.00
Sri Lanka	1992-93	5	1217	51	591	15	39.40	-	-	4/71	81.13
West Indies	1992-93	13	2781	114	1313	47	27.94	1	-	7/52	59.17
New Zealand	1992-93	6	1863	122	561	35	16.03	1	-	6/31	53.22
England	1993	11	4176	262	1426	61	23.38	3	1	8/71	77.31
South Africa	1993-94	9	2994	179	925	44	21.02	2	1	7/56	68.04
Pakistan	1994-95	6	1780	102	702	37	18.97	3	1	7/23	48.10

INNINGS OF MATCH COMPARISON

	Balls	Mdns	Runs	Wkts	Avrge	5	10	Best	Stk/Rt
First Innings	4997	246	1989	66	30.14	2	-	7/23	75.71
Second Innings	3016	164	1246	51	24.43	2	-	7/56	59.13
Third Innings	2282	142	820	43	19.07	3	-	8/71	53.06
Fourth Innings	4924	287	1691	80	21.14	3	-	6/31	61.55

BOWLING

Series	Opponent	Venue	M	Balls	Mdns	Runs	Wkts	Avrge	5	10	Best	Stk/Rt
1991-92	India	Australia	2	408	9	228	1	228.00	-	-	1/150	408.00
1992-93	Sri Lanka	Sri Lanka	2	229	8	158	3	52.67	-	-	3/11	76.33
1992-93	West Indies	Australia	4	650	23	313	10	31.30	1	-	7/52	65.00
1992-93	New Zealand	New Zealand	3	954	73	256	17	15.06	-	-	4/8	56.11
1993	England	England	6	2639	178	877	34	25.79	1	-	5/82	77.61
1993-94	New Zealand	Australia	3	909	49	305	18	16.94	1	-	6/31	50.50
1993-94	South Africa	Australia	3	1051	63	307	18	17.06	2	1	7/56	58.38
1993-94	South Africa	South Africa	3	1145	69	336	15	22.40	-	-	4/86	76.33
1994-95	Pakistan	Pakistan	3	1090	50	504	18	28.00	2	-	6/136	60.55
1994-95	England	Australia	5	1537	84	549	27	20.33	2	1	8/71	56.92
1994-95	West Indies	West Indies	4	828	35	406	15	27.07	-	-	4/70	55.20
1995-96	Pakistan	Australia	3	690	52	198	19	10.42	1	1	7/23	36.31
1995-96	Sri Lanka	Australia	3	988	43	433	12	36.08	-	-	4/71	82.33
1996-97	West Indies	Australia	5	1303	56	594	22	27.00	-	-	4/95	59.22
1996-97	South Africa	South Africa	3	798	47	282	11	25.64	-	-	4/43	72.54
Total			52	15219	839	5746	240	23.94	10	3	8/71	63.41

FIFTY WICKET COMPARISON

Date		M	Balls	Mdns	Runs	Wkts	Avrge	5	10	Best	Stk/Rt
July 2	1993	14	3421	194	1325	50	26.50	1	-	7/52	68.42
February 1	1994	23	6832	402	2444	100	24.44	5	1	7/52	68.32
December 27	1994	31	9650	559	3445	150	22.96	9	2	8/71	64.33
December 12	1995	42	12460	706	4600	200	23.00	10	3	8/71	62.30

VENUES

	Debut	M	Balls	Mdns	Runs	Wkts	Avrge	5	10	Best	Stk/Rt
In Australia												
Sydney	1991-92	6	2046	101	811	30	27.03	2	1	7/56	68.20
Adelaide	1991-92	6	1542	75	629	17	37.00	-	-	4/31	90.70
Melbourne	1992-93	5	1231	55	469	26	18.04	2	-	7/52	47.34
Perth	1992-93	5	1007	44	459	11	41.73	-	-	3/75	91.54
Hobart	1993-94	2	227	14	67	9	7.44	1	-	6/31	25.22
Brisbane	1993-94	4	1483	90	492	34	14.47	2	2	8/71	43.61
In Sri Lanka												
Colombo	1992-93	1	163	5	118	3	39.33	-	-	3/11	54.33
Moratuwa	1992-93	1	66	3	40	-	-	-	-	-	-
In New Zealand												
Christchurch	1992-93	1	288	19	86	7	12.29	-	-	4/63	41.14
Wellington	1992-93	1	414	34	108	4	27.00	-	-	2/49	103.50
Auckland	1992-93	1	252	20	62	6	10.33	-	-	4/8	42.00
In England												
Manchester	1993	1	438	36	137	8	17.13	-	-	4/51	54.75
Lord's	1993	1	503	29	159	8	19.88	-	-	4/57	62.87
Nottingham	1993	1	540	38	182	6	30.33	-	-	3/74	90.00
Leeds	1993	1	378	25	106	1	106.00	-	-	1/43	378.00
Birmingham	1993	1	420	30	145	6	24.17	1	-	5/82	70.00
The Oval	1993	1	360	20	148	5	29.60	-	-	3/78	72.00
In South Africa												
Johannesburg	1993-94	2	687	42	239	11	21.73	-	-	4/43	62.45
Cape Town	1993-94	1	462	31	116	6	19.33	-	-	3/38	77.00
Durban	1993-94	1	330	20	92	4	23.00	-	-	4/92	82.50
Centurion	1996-97	1	216	11	89	-	-	-	-	-	-
Port Elizabeth	1996-97	1	248	12	82	5	16.40	-	-	3/62	49.60
In Pakistan												
Karachi	1994-95	1	379	22	150	8	18.75	1	-	5/89	47.37
Rawalpindi	1994-95	1	280	14	114	1	114.00	-	-	1/58	280.00
Lahore	1994-95	1	431	14	240	9	26.67	1	-	6/136	47.88
In West Indies												
Bridgetown	1994-95	1	231	7	121	5	24.20	-	-	3/64	46.20
St John's	1994-95	1	210	9	101	3	33.67	-	-	3/83	70.00
Port-of-Spain	1994-95	1	95	5	42	1	42.00	-	-	1/16	95.00
Kingston	1994-95	1	292	14	142	6	23.67	-	-	4/70	48.66

RECORD IN EACH COUNTRY

Country	Debut	M	Balls	Mdns	Runs	Wkts	Avrge	5	10	Best	Stk/Rt
Australia	1991-92	28	7536	379	2927	127	23.05	7	3	8/71	59.33
Sri Lanka	1992-93	2	229	8	158	3	52.67	-	-	3/11	76.33
New Zealand	1992-93	3	954	73	256	17	15.06	-	-	4/8	56.11
England	1993	6	2639	178	877	34	25.79	1	-	5/82	77.61
South Africa	1993-94	6	1943	116	618	26	23.77	-	-	4/43	74.73
Pakistan	1994-95	3	1090	50	504	18	28.00	2	-	6/136	60.55
West Indies	1994-95	4	828	35	406	15	27.07	-	-	4/70	55.20

WICKETS TAKEN

How Out	Wkts	%
Caught	137	57.08
(ct MA Taylor)	35	14.58
(ct IA Healy)	23	9.58
(ct ME Waugh)	15	6.25
(cgt and bwd)	12	5.00
(ct DC Boon)	11	4.58
L.B.W.	47	19.58
Bowled	44	18.33
Stumped	12	5.00
(st IA Healy)	11	4.58
(st PA Emery)	1	0.41

BATSMEN DISMISSED

Postion		Wkts	%
Openers		36	15.00
Number	3	20	8.33
Number	4	24	10.00
Number	5	25	10.41
Number	6	23	9.58
Number	7	20	8.33
Number	8	25	10.41
Number	9	21	8.75
Number	10	29	12.08
Number	11	17	7.08
Number	1-6	128	53.33
Number	7-11	112	46.66

Batsman		Wkts
MA Atherton	(England)	6
GA Gooch	(England)	6
AJ Stewart	(England)	6
GP Thorpe	(England)	6
CA Walsh	(West Indies)	5
DJ Richardson	(South Africa)	5

FIVE WICKETS IN AN INNINGS

Wkts	Opponent	Venue	Series
7/52	West Indies	Melbourne	1992-93
5/82	England	Birmingham	1993
6/31	New Zealand	Hobart	1993-94
7/56	South Africa	Sydney	1993-94
5/72	South Africa	Sydney	1993-94
5/89	Pakistan	Karachi	1994-95
8/71	England	Brisbane	1994-95
6/64	England	Melbourne	1994-95
7/23	Pakistan	Brisbane	1995-96

INNINGS BY INNINGS

Tst	Inn	Venue	Ovrs	Md	Rns	Wk	Batsman	How Out	Wkt	Balls	Mds	Runs	Avrge	5	10	Stk/Rt
1991-92 v India in Australia																
1	1	Sydney	40.3	7	133	1	RJ Shastri	ct DM Jones	1	243	7	133	133.00	-	-	243.00
			45.0	7	150	1			1	270	7	150	150.00	-	-	270.00
2	2	Adelaide	7.0	1	18	-			1	312	8	168	168.00	-	-	312.00
	3		16.0	1	60	-			1	408	9	228	228.00	-	-	408.00
1992-93 v Sri Lanka in Sri Lanka																
3	4	Colombo (SSC)	22.0	2	107	-			1	540	11	335	335.00	-	-	540.00
	5		3.1	1	11	1	GP Wickramasinghe	ct ME Waugh	2	559	12	346	173.00	-	-	279.50
			4.5	2	11	2	SD Anurasiri	ct ME Waugh	3	589	13	346	115.33	-	-	196.33
			5.1	3	11	3	MAWR Madurasinghe	ct GRJ Matthews	4	571	14	346	86.50	-	-	142.75
4	6	Moratuwa	11.0	3	40	-			4	637	17	386	96.50	-	-	159.25
1992-93 v West Indies in Australia																
5	7	Melbourne	23.3	6	65	1	CEL Ambrose	ct CJ McDermott	5	778	23	451	90.20	-	-	155.60
			24.0	7	65	1			5	781	24	451	90.20	-	-	156.20
	8		8.5	-	32	1	RB Richardson	bowled	6	834	24	483	80.50	-	-	139.00
			12.4	2	41	2	KLT Arthurton	stp IA Healy	7	857	26	492	70.28	-	-	122.42
			14.3	3	45	3	CL Hooper	ct MR Whitney	8	868	27	496	62.00	-	-	108.50
			18.1	5	49	4	PV Simmons	ct DC Boon	9	890	29	500	55.55	-	-	98.88
			21.4	8	51	5	D Williams	ct ME Waugh	10	911	32	502	50.20	1	-	91.10
			23.1	8	52	6	IR Bishop	ct MA Taylor	11	920	32	502	45.63	1	-	83.63
			23.2	8	52	7	CA Walsh	ct MG Hughes	12	921	32	503	41.92	1	-	76.75
6	9	Sydney	33.3	4	99	1	CL Hooper	bowled	13	1122	36	602	46.30	1	-	86.30
			41.0	6	116	1			13	1167	38	619	47.62	1	-	89.77
7	10	Adelaide	2.0	-	11	-			13	1179	38	630	48.46	1	-	90.69
	11		4.2	2	17	1	RB Richardson	ct IA Healy	14	1205	38	647	46.21	1	-	86.07
			6.0	2	18	1			14	1215	40	648	46.29	1	-	86.79
8	12	Perth	12.0	-	51	-			14	1287	40	699	49.93	1	-	91.93
1992-93 v New Zealand in New Zealand																
9	13	Christchurch	8.4	7	2	1	AH Jones	lbw	15	1339	47	701	46.73	1	-	89.26
			11.3	7	6	2	KR Rutherford	ct DC Boon	16	1356	47	705	44.06	1	-	84.75
			21.5	12	23	3	MB Owens	lbw	17	1418	52	722	42.47	1	-	83.41
			22.0	12	23	3			17	1419	52	722	42.47	1	-	83.47
	14		4.1	1	5	1	CL Cairns	ct MA Taylor	18	1444	53	727	40.38	1	-	80.22
			9.5	3	14	2	AC Parore	ct DC Boon	19	1503	55	736	38.73	1	-	79.12
			15.5	4	24	3	DN Patel	bowled	20	1509	56	746	37.30	1	-	75.45
			22.3	5	48	4	KR Rutherford	ct IA Healy	21	1554	57	770	36.66	1	-	74.00
			26.0	7	63	4			21	1575	59	785	37.38	1	-	75.00
10	15	Wellington	28.5	9	59	2	W Watson	ct MA Taylor	22	1748	68	844	36.70	1	-	76.00
			29.0	9	59	2	MB Owens	bowled	23	1749	68	844	36.70	1	-	76.04
	16		19.2	11	29	1	AH Jones	lbw	24	1865	79	873	36.37	1	-	77.70
			29.1	19	37	2	TE Blain	ct IA Healy	25	1924	87	881	35.24	1	-	76.96
			40.0	25	49	2			25	1989	93	893	35.72	1	-	79.56
11	17	Auckland	1.2	1	0	1	KR Rutherford	ct MA Taylor	26	1997	94	893	34.34	1	-	76.80
			8.3	6	5	2	DN Patel	ct IA Healy	27	2040	99	898	33.25	1	-	75.55
			9.4	7	5	3	CZ Harris	ct MA Taylor	28	2047	100	898	32.07	1	-	73.10
			15.0	12	8	4			29	2079	105	901	31.07	1	-	71.69
	18		11.2	5	17	1	MD Crowe	ct JL Langer	30	2147	110	918	30.60	1	-	71.56
			16.1	5	24	2	AH Jones	bowled	31	2176	110	925	29.83	1	-	70.19
			27.0	8	54	2			31	2241	113	955	30.81	1	-	72.29

Tst	Inn	Venue	Ovrs	Md	Rns	Wk	Batsman	How Out	Wkt	Balls	Mds	Runs	Avrge	5	10	Stk/Rt
1993 v England in England																
12	19	Manchester	0.1	-	0	1	MW Gatting	bowled	32	2242	113	955	29.84	1	-	70.06
			1.1	-	4	2	RA Smith	ct MA Taylor	33	2248	113	959	29.06	1	-	68.12
			9.0	5	14	3	GA Gooch	ct BP Julian	34	2295	118	969	28.50	1	-	67.50
			21.2	7	51	4	AR Caddick	ct IA Healy	35	2369	120	1006	28.74	1	-	67.68
			24.0	10	51	4			35	2385	123	1006	28.74	1	-	68.14
	20		5.5	4	4	1	MA Atherton	ct MA Taylor	36	2420	127	1010	28.05	1	-	67.22
			22.4	12	46	2	RA Smith	bowled	37	2521	135	1052	28.43	1	-	68.13
			37.2	18	70	3	AJ Stewart	ct IA Healy	38	2607	141	1076	28.31	1	-	68.60
			45.2	25	74	4	CC Lewis	ct MA Taylor	39	2657	158	1080	27.69	1	-	68.12
			49.0	26	86	4			39	2679	149	1092	28.00	1	-	68.69
13	21	Lord's	14.0	3	35	1	CC Lewis	lbw	40	2763	152	1127	28.17	1	-	69.07
			20.5	3	45	2	NA Foster	ct AR Border	41	2804	152	1137	27.73	1	-	68.39
			23.0	4	50	3	MA Atherton	bowled	42	2817	153	1142	27.19	1	-	67.07
			29.2	8	54	4	PM Such	ct MA Taylor	43	2855	157	1146	26.65	1	-	66.39
			35.0	12	57	4			43	2889	161	1149	26.72	1	-	67.19
	22		5.0	2	8	1	GA Gooch	ct IA Healy	44	2919	163	1157	26.29	1	-	66.34
			34.0	11	64	2	MW Gatting	lbw	45	3093	172	1213	26.95	1	-	68.73
			48.4	17	102	3	PM Such	bowled	46	3181	178	1251	26.62	1	-	69.15
			48.5	17	102	4	PCR Tufnell	bowled	47	3182	178	1251	26.62	1	-	67.70
14	23	Nottingham	3.4	2	5	1	MA Atherton	ct DC Boon	48	3204	180	1256	26.16	1	-	66.75
			14.4	6	36	2	AJ Stewart	ct ME Waugh	49	3270	186	1287	26.26	1	-	66.73
			39.5	16	74	3	N Hussain	ct DC Boon	50	3421	194	1325	26.50	1	-	68.42
			40.0	17	74	3			50	3422	195	1325	26.50	1	-	68.44
	24		7.0	2	25	1	RA Smith	ct IA Healy	51	3464	197	1350	26.47	1	-	67.92
			8.1	2	29	2	MN Lathwell	lbw	52	3471	197	1354	26.02	1	-	66.75
			39.0	18	77	3	GA Gooch	ct MA Taylor	53	3656	213	1402	26.45	1	-	68.98
			50.0	21	108	3			53	3722	216	1433	27.04	1	-	70.23
15	25	Leeds	22.1	8	43	1	MJ McCague	ct MA Taylor	54	3855	224	1476	27.33	1	-	71.38
			23.0	9	43	1			54	3860	225	1476	27.33	1	-	71.48
	26		40.0	16	63	-			54	4100	241	1539	28.50	1	-	75.93
16	27	Birmingham	6.0	2	21	1	GP Thorpe	ct IA Healy	55	4136	243	1560	28.36	1	-	75.20
			21.0	7	63	1			55	4226	248	1602	29.13	1	-	76.84
	28		3.4	2	6	1	MA Atherton	ct AR Border	56	4248	250	1608	28.71	1	-	75.85
			15.0	7	33	2	RA Smith	lbw	57	4316	257	1635	28.68	1	-	75.71
			17.2	8	34	3	GA Gooch	bowled	58	4330	256	1636	28.20	1	-	74.65
			20.3	9	39	4	AJ Stewart	lbw	59	4349	257	1641	27.81	1	-	73.71
			46.0	23	68	5	GP Thorpe	stp IA Healy	60	4502	271	1670	27.83	2	-	75.03
			49.0	23	82	5			60	4520	271	1684	28.07	2	-	75.33
17	29	The Oval	2.5	1	9	1	MP Maynard	b owled	61	4537	272	1693	27.75	2	-	74.37
			10.3	2	36	2	N Hussain	ct MA Taylor	62	4583	273	1720	27.74	2	-	73.91
			20.0	5	70	2			62	4640	276	1754	28.29	2	-	74.84
	30		15.3	6	33	1	GA Gooch	ct IA Healy	63	4733	282	1787	28.36	2	-	28.36
			33.0	13	66	2	SL Watkin	lbw	64	4838	289	1820	28.43	2	-	75.59
			39.2	14	78	3	PM Such	lbw	65	4876	290	1832	28.18	2	-	75.01
			40.0	15	78	3			65	4880	291	1832	28.18	2	-	75.08
1993-94 v New Zealand in Australia																
18	31	Perth	33.3	4	86	1	CL Cairns	bowled	66	5081	295	1918	29.06	2	-	76.98
			37.1	6	90	1			66	5103	297	1922	29.12	2	-	77.32
	32		13.0	6	23	-			66	5181	303	1945	29.47	2	-	78.50
19	33	Hobart	8.1	1	16	1	DN Patel	ct MA Taylor	67	5230	304	1961	29.26	2	-	78.05
			14.5	4	30	2	ML Su'a	ct MA Taylor	68	5270	307	1975	29.04	2	-	77.50

Tst	Inn	Venue	Ovrs	Md	Rns	Wk	Batsman	How Out	Wkt	Balls	Mds	Runs	Avrge	5	10	Stk/Rt

1993-94 v New Zealand in Australia (cont.)

Tst	Inn	Venue	Ovrs	Md	Rns	Wk	Batsman	How Out	Wkt	Balls	Mds	Runs	Avrge	5	10	Stk/Rt
19	33	Hobart (cont.)	15.5	4	31	3	SB Doull	lbw	69	5276	307	1976	28.63	2	-	76.46
			18.0	5	36	3			69	5289	308	1981	28.71	2	-	76.65
	34		10.1	5	15	1	BA Pocock	stp IA Healy	70	5350	313	1996	28.51	2	-	76.42
			12.4	5	25	2	KR Rutherford	bowled	71	5365	313	2006	28.25	2	-	75.56
			17.4	7	28	3	ML Su'a	bowled	72	5395	315	2009	27.90	2	-	74.93
			18.0	8	28	4	DK Morrison	bowled	73	5397	316	2009	27.52	2	-	73.93
			19.1	9	28	5	TE Blain	ct SK Warne	74	5404	317	2009	27.14	3	-	73.02
			19.5	9	31	6	SB Doull	ct TBA May	75	5408	317	2012	26.83	3	-	72.11
20	35	Brisbane	8.3	4	16	1	AH Jones	bowled	76	5459	321	2028	26.68	3	-	71.82
			20.0	9	45	2	CL Cairns	ct SK Warne	77	5528	321	2057	26.71	3	-	71.79
			23.1	12	49	3	DK Morrison	ct IA Healy	78	5547	329	2061	26.42	3	-	71.11
			28.3	12	66	4	RP De Groen	ct AR Border	79	5579	329	2078	26.30	3	-	70.62
	36		6.5	2	8	1	AH Jones	ct AR Border	80	5620	331	2086	26.07	3	-	70.25
			7.3	3	8	2	BA Young	bowled	81	5624	334	2086	25.75	3	-	69.43
			28.0	10	43	3	DN Patel	bowled	82	5747	339	2121	25.86	3	-	70.08
			33.1	10	55	4	SB Doull	ct MA Taylor	83	5778	339	2133	25.69	3	-	69.61
			35.0	11	59	4			83	5789	340	2137	25.75	3	-	69.75

1993-94 v South Africa in Australia

Tst	Inn	Venue	Ovrs	Md	Rns	Wk	Batsman	How Out	Wkt	Balls	Mds	Runs	Avrge	5	10	Stk/Rt
21	37	Melbourne	18.0	5	42	1	WJ Cronje	ct DC Boon	84	5897	345	2179	25.94	3	-	70.20
			31.0	8	63	1			84	5975	348	2200	26.19	3	-	71.13
22	38	Sydney	12.0	4	28	1	DJ Cullinan	bowled	85	6047	352	2228	26.21	3	-	71.14
			16.0	5	37	2	JN Rhodes	lbw	86	6071	353	2237	26.01	3	-	70.59
			16.2	5	37	3	G Kirsten	stp IA Healy	87	6073	353	2237	25.71	3	-	69.80
			17.3	5	42	4	DJ Richardson	ct MA Taylor	88	6080	353	2242	25.47	3	-	69.09
			18.5	6	42	5	KC Wessels	ct SK Warne	89	6088	354	2242	25.19	4	-	68.40
			19.3	7	42	6	CR Matthews	ct MA Taylor	90	6092	355	2242	24.91	4	-	67.68
			24.4	8	50	7	PL Symcox	bowled	91	6123	356	2250	24.72	4	-	67.28
			27.0	8	56	7			91	6137	356	2256	24.79	4	-	67.43
	39		18.5	9	31	1	KC Wessels	bowled	92	6250	365	2287	24.85	4	-	67.93
			19.3	9	31	2	DJ Cullinan	lbw	93	6254	365	2287	24.59	4	-	67.24
			33.4	14	59	3	CR Matthews	ct ME Waugh	94	6339	370	2315	24.62	4	-	67.43
			35.4	15	64	4	PS De Villiers	lbw	95	6347	371	2320	24.42	4	-	66.81
			42.0	17	72	5	AA Donald	ct IA Healy	96	6389	373	2328	24.25	5	1	66.55
23	40	Adelaide	43.3	14	84	1	PN Kirsten	ct ME Waugh	97	6650	387	2412	24.86	5	1	68.55
			44.2	15	85	1			97	6655	388	2413	24.87	5	1	68.60
	41		2.4	1	1	1	WJ Cronje	lbw	98	6405	389	2414	24.63	5	1	65.35
			4.2	2	2	2	G Kirsten	bowled	99	6681	390	2415	24.39	5	1	67.48
			29.3	14	31	3	BM McMillan	lbw	100	6832	402	2444	24.44	5	1	68.32
			30.5	15	31	4	RP Snell	ct SK Warne	101	6840	403	2444	24.20	5	1	67.72

1993-94 v South Africa in South Africa

Tst	Inn	Venue	Ovrs	Md	Rns	Wk	Batsman	How Out	Wkt	Balls	Mds	Runs	Avrge	5	10	Stk/Rt
24	42	Johannesburg	4.2	-	20	1	DJ Richardson	lbw	102	6866	403	2464	24.15	5	1	67.31
			14.0	4	42	1			102	6924	407	2486	24.37	5	1	67.88
	43		0.3	-	0	1	AC Hudson	bowled	103	6927	407	2486	24.13	5	1	67.25
			17.3	4	30	2	KC Wessels	ct AR Border	104	7029	411	2516	24.19	5	1	67.58
			34.2	9	57	3	DJ Richardson	ct AR Border	105	7130	416	2543	24.21	5	1	67.90
			37.3	11	59	4	BM McMillan	bowled	106	7149	418	2545	24.00	5	1	67.44
			44.5	14	86	4			106	7193	421	2572	24.26	5	1	67.86
25	44	Cape Town	26.3	8	42	1	PN Kirsten	lbw	107	7352	429	2614	24.42	5	1	68.71
			40.5	14	69	2	BM McMillan	bowled	108	7438	435	2641	24.45	5	1	68.87
			42.1	15	73	3	PS De Villiers	ct MA Taylor	109	7446	436	2645	24.26	5	1	68.31
			47.0	18	78	3			109	7475	439	2650	24.31	5	1	68.58

Tst	Inn	Venue	Ovrs	Md	Rns	Wk	Batsman	How Out	Wkt	Balls	Mds	Runs	Avrge	5	10	Stk/Rt
1993-94 v South Africa in South Africa (cont.)																
25	45	C'Town (cont.)	0.4	-	0	1	G Kirsten	lbw	110	7479	439	2650	24.10	5	1	67.99
			14.2	8	18	2	PN Kirsten	ct MA Taylor	111	7561	447	2668	24.03	5	1	68.11
			14.5	8	18	3	PS De Villiers	lbw	112	7564	447	2668	23.82	5	1	67.53
			30.0	13	38	3			112	7655	452	2688	24.00	5	1	68.35
26	46	Durban	20.1	8	32	1	WJ Cronje	ct SR Waugh	113	7776	460	2720	24.07	5	1	68.81
			36.0	13	64	2	JN Rhodes	lbw	114	7871	465	2752	24.14	5	1	69.04
			51.1	18	89	3	DJ Richardson	ct PR Reiffel	115	7962	470	2777	24.14	5	1	69.23
			54.5	19	92	4	CR Matthews	lbw	116	7984	471	2780	23.96	5	1	68.82
			55.0	20	92	4			116	7985	472	2780	23.96	5	1	68.84
1994-95 v Pakistan in Pakistan																
27	47	Karachi	2.5	-	14	1	Aamir Sohail	ct MG Bevan	117	8002	472	2794	23.88	5	1	68.39
			16.0	5	46	2	Inzamam-ul-Haq	ct MA Taylor	118	8098	477	2840	24.06	5	1	68.62
			17.0	6	46	3	Rashid Latif	ct MA Taylor	119	8087	478	2840	23.86	5	1	67.95
			27.0	10	61	3			119	8147	482	2841	23.87	5	1	68.46
	48					1	Zahid Fazal	ct DC Boon	120							
						2	Akram Raja	lbw	121							
						3	Wasim Akram	ct SK Warne	122							
						4	Waqar Younis	ct IA Healy	123							
			36.1	12	89	5			123	8364	494	2930	23.63	6	1	67.45
28	49	Rawalpindi	15.0	5	44	1	Inzamam-ul-Haq	lbw	125							
			21.4	8	58	1			125	8494	502	2988	23.90	6	1	67.95
			25.0	6	56	-			125	8644	508	3044	24.35	6	1	69.15
29	50	Lahore	2.3	1	1	-	Saeed Anwar	bowled	126	8653	509	3045	24.16	6	1	68.67
			21.2	5	65	2	Basit Ali	ct ME Waugh	127	8772	513	3109	24.48	6	1	69.07
			28.3	8	102	3	Ijaz Ahmed	ct DC Boon	128	8812	516	3146	24.57	6	1	68.84
			29.0	9	102	4	Akram Raza	bowled	129	8815	517	3146	24.38	6	1	68.33
			40.0	12	126	5	Aaqib Javed	ct ME Waugh	130	8884	520	3170	24.38	7	1	68.33
			41.5	12	136	6	Mohsin Kamal	lbw	131	8895	520	3180	24.27	7	1	67.90
	51		23.1	1	88	1	Aamir Sohail	ct PA Emery	132	9034	521	3268	24.75	7	1	68.43
			27.0	2	95	2	Akram Raza	lbw	133	9057	522	3275	24.62	7	1	68.09
			27.5	2	97	3	Aaqib Javed	bowled	134	9062	522	3277	24.45	7	1	67.62
			30.0	2	104	3			134	9075	522	3284	24.51	7	1	67.72
1994-95 v England in Australia																
30	52	Brisbane	7.3	2	7	1	GP Thorpe	ct SK Warne	135	9120	524	3291	24.37	7	1	67.55
			18.2	6	34	2	PAJ DeFreitas	ct IA Healy	136	9185	528	3318	24.39	7	1	67.53
			21.2	7	39	3	PCR Tufnell	ct MA Taylor	137	9203	529	3323	24.26	7	1	67.18
	53		1.5	-	9	1	AJ Stewart	bowled	138	9214	529	3332	24.14	7	1	66.76
			2.3	-	10	2	MA Atherton	lbw	139	9218	529	3333	23.97	7	1	66.31
			30.2	12	49	3	GP Thorpe	bowled	140	9385	541	3372	24.08	7	1	67.03
			31.1	13	49	4	GA Hick	ct IA Healy	141	9390	542	3372	23.91	7	1	66.59
			45.5	19	69	5	GA Gooch	ct IA Healy	142	9478	548	3392	23.88	8	1	66.74
			46.1	20	69	6	PAJ DeFreitas	bowled	143	9480	549	3392	23.72	8	1	66.29
			46.2	20	69	7	MJ McCague	lbw	144	9481	549	3392	23.55	8	2	65.84
			50.2	22	71	8	D Gough	ct ME Waugh	145	9505	551	3394	23.41	8	2	65.55
31	54	Melbourne	10.3	3	21	1	MA Atherton	lbw	146	9568	554	3415	23.39	8	2	65.53
			13.1	5	21	2	GP Thorpe	ct ME Waugh	147	9584	559	3415	23.23	8	2	65.19
			17.0	6	29	3	MW Gatting	ct SR Waugh	148	9607	557	3423	23.12	8	2	64.91
			21.3	8	35	4	SJ Rhodes	ct ME Waugh	149	9634	559	3429	23.01	8	2	64.65
			24.1	8	51	5	AJ Stewart	ct SK Warne	150	9650	559	3445	22.96	9	2	64.33
			27.0	8	64	6	PAJ DeFreitas	stp IA Healy	151	9667	559	3458	22.90	9	2	64.01
			27.4	8	64	6			151	9671	559	3458	22.90	9	2	64.05

Tst	Inn	Venue	Ovrs	Md	Rns	Wk	Batsman	How Out	Wkt	Balls	Mds	Runs	Avrge	5	10	Stk/Rt
1994-95 v England in Australia (cont.)															
31	55	Melb'ne (cont.)	12.4	6	16	1	PAJ DeFreitas	lbw	152	9747	565	3474	22.85	9	2	64.12
			12.5	6	16	2	D Gough	ct IA Healy	153	9748	565	3474	22.70	9	2	63.71
			13.0	6	16	3	DE Malcolm	ct DC Boon	154	9749	565	3474	22.56	9	2	63.31
32	56	Sydney	33.3	10	83	1	DE Malcolm	bowled	155	9950	575	3557	22.94	9	2	64.19
			36.0	10	88	1			155	9965	575	3562	22.98	9	2	64.29
	57		16.0	2	48	-			155	10061	577	3610	23.29	9	2	64.91
33	58	Adelaide	14.0	3	48	1	GP Thorpe	ct MA Taylor	156	10145	580	3658	23.44	9	2	65.03
			21.3	5	59	2	JP Crawley	bowled	157	10190	582	3669	23.36	9	2	64.90
			31.0	9	72	2			157	10247	586	3682	23.45	9	2	65.27
	59		20.0	7	44	1	SJ Rhodes	ct DW Fleming	158	10367	593	3726	23.58	9	2	65.61
			30.5	9	82	2	PCR Tufnell	lbw	159	10432	595	3764	23.67	9	2	65.61
34	60	Perth	15.3	4	45	1	GP Thorpe	stp IA Healy	160	10525	599	3809	23.80	9	2	65.78
			19.1	7	47	2	MR Ramprakash	bowled	161	10547	602	3811	23.67	9	2	65.50
			23.0	8	58	2			161	10570	603	3822	23.74	9	2	65.65
	61		7.0	3	11	-			161	10612	606	3833	23.81	9	2	65.91
1994-95 v West Indies in West Indies															
35	62	Bridgetown	9.2	2	48	1	WKM Benjamin	ct MA Taylor	162	10668	608	3881	23.95	9	2	65.85
			11.3	2	56	2	CA Walsh	ct SR Waugh	163	10681	608	3889	23.85	9	2	65.52
			12.0	2	57	2			163	10684	608	3890	23.87	9	2	65.55
	63		5.1	1	7	1	SL Campbell	ct SR Waugh	164	10715	609	3897	23.76	9	2	65.33
			19.3	2	42	2	JR Murray	ct SR Waugh	165	10801	610	3932	23.83	9	2	65.46
			26.3	5	64	3	KCG Benjamin	bowled	166	10843	613	3954	23.82	9	2	65.32
36	64	St John's	7.1	3	10	1	SC Williams	ct DC Boon	167	10886	616	3964	23.73	9	2	65.18
			18.4	8	54	2	JC Adams	lbw	168	10955	621	4008	23.85	9	2	65.20
			26.0	8	82	3	KLT Arthurton	ct MA Taylor	169	10999	621	4036	23.88	9	2	65.08
			28.0	9	83	3			169	11011	622	4037	23.89	9	2	65.15
	65		7.0	-	18	-			169	11053	622	4055	23.99	9	2	65.40
37	66	Port-of-Spain	7.1	4	12	1	WKM Benjamin	ct MJ Slater	170	11096	626	4067	23.92	9	2	65.27
			12.0	5	16	1			170	11125	627	4071	23.95	9	2	65.44
	67		3.5	-	26	-			170	11148	627	4097	24.10	9	2	65.58
38	68	Kingston	5.2	-	26	1	BC Lara	ct IA Healy	171	11180	627	4123	24.11	9	2	65.38
			22.4	5	70	2	CO Browne	ct DC Boon	172	11284	632	4167	24.22	9	2	65.60
			25.0	6	72	2			172	11298	633	4169	24.24	9	2	65.69
	69		15.3	7	40	1	KLT Arthurton	lbw	173	11391	640	4209	24.32	9	2	65.84
			16.3	7	44	2	CEL Ambrose	stp IA Healy	174	11397	640	4213	24.21	9	2	17.80
			22.1	7	63	3	CA Walsh	ct GS Blewett	175	11431	640	4232	24.18	9	2	65.32
			23.4	8	70	4	KCG Benjamin	ct MA Taylor	176	11440	641	4239	24.09	9	2	65.00
1995-96 v Pakistan in Australia															
39	70	Brisbane	3.2	1	7	1	Rameez Raja	ct MA Taylor	177	11460	642	4246	23.98	9	2	64.74
			7.0	3	13	2	Aamir Sohail	stp IA Healy	178	11482	644	4252	23.88	9	2	64.50
			9.2	5	13	3	Inzamam-ul-Haq	ct SR Waugh	179	11496	646	4252	23.75	9	2	64.22
			11.5	7	17	4	Moin Khan	ct CJ McDermott	180	11511	648	4256	23.64	9	2	63.95
			12.3	7	17	5	Basit Ali	ct MA Taylor	181	11515	648	4256	23.51	10	2	63.61
			14.4	8	21	6	Wasim Akram	ct DC Boon	182	11528	649	4260	23.40	10	2	63.34
			16.1	9	23	7	Mohammad Akram	ct GS Blewett	183	11537	650	4262	23.29	10	2	63.04
	71		22.1	6	53	1	Wasim Akram	ct MJ Slater	184	11670	656	4315	23.45	10	2	63.42
			22.5	6	53	2	Salim Malik	ct CJ McDermott	185	11674	656	4315	23.32	10	2	63.10
			27.1	10	54	3	Waqar Younis	lbw	186	11700	660	4316	23.20	10	2	62.90
			27.5	10	54	4	Mohammad Akram	Lbw	187	11704	660	4316	23.08	10	3	62.59
40	72	Hobart	-	-	-	-			187	11704	660	4316	23.08	10	3	62.59
	73		-	-	-	-			187	11704	660	4316	23.08	10	3	62.59

Tst Inn	Venue	Ovrs	Md	Rns	Wk	Batsman	How Out	Wkt	Balls	Mds	Runs	Avrge	5	10	Stk/Rt
1995-96 v Pakistan in Australia (cont.)															
41 74	Sydney	5.1	3	6	1	Rameez Raja	ct MJ Slater	188	11735	663	4322	22.98	10	3	62.42
		14.0	8	21	2	Inzamam-ul-Haq	ct IA Healy	189	11788	668	4337	22.94	10	3	62.37
		32.2	18	55	3	Ijaz Ahmed	ct GD McGrath	190	11898	678	4371	23.00	10	3	62.62
		33.3	19	55	4	Mushtaq Ahmed	ct CJ McDermott	191	11905	659	4371	22.88	10	3	62.32
		34.0	20	55	4			191	11908	680	4371	22.88	10	3	62.35
75		5.5	-	10	1	Ijaz Ahmed	lbw	192	11943	680	4381	22.81	10	3	62.20
		10.3	2	24	2	Rameez Raja	ct ME Waugh	193	11971	682	4395	22.77	10	3	62.02
		17.0	6	28	3	Basit Ali	bowled	194	12010	686	4399	22.67	10	3	61.90
		32.4	10	60	4	Rashid Latif	lbw	195	12104	690	4431	22.72	10	3	62.07
		37.0	13	66	4			195	12130	693	4437	22.75	10	3	62.21
1995-96 v Sri Lanka in Australia															
42 76	Perth	2.0	1	4	1	PA De Silva	ct SK Warne	196	12142	694	4441	22.65	10	3	61.94
		22.5	5	61	2	RS Kaluwitharana	ct MA Taylor	197	12267	698	4498	22.83	10	3	62.26
		24.1	6	66	3	WPUJC Vaas	ct IA Healy	198	12275	699	4503	22.74	10	3	61.99
		27.0	7	75	3			198	12292	700	4512	22.79	10	3	62.08
77		7.0	3	13	1	PA De Silva	ct RT Ponting	199	12334	703	4525	22.72	10	3	61.97
		28.0	6	88	2	HP Tillakaratne	ct RT Ponting	200	12460	706	4600	23.00	10	3	62.30
		29.4	6	96	3	WPUCJ Vaas	ct IA Healy	201	12470	706	4608	22.93	10	3	62.04
43 78	Melbourne	13.3	5	35	1	HP Tillakaratne	ct MA Taylor	202	12551	711	4643	22.98	10	3	62.13
		18.0	5	49	1			202	12578	711	4657	23.05	10	3	62.27
79		7.5	2	13	1	UC Haturusinghe	lbw	203	12625	713	4670	23.00	10	3	62.19
		16.1	3	36	2	RS Kaluwitharan	stp IA Healy	204	12675	714	4693	23.00	10	3	62.13
		36.1	9	71	3	GP Wickramasinghe	stp IA Healy	205	12795	720	4728	23.06	10	3	62.41
		36.2	9	71	4	M Muralidaran	ct MA Taylor	206	12796	720	4728	22.95	10	3	62.11
		37.0	10	71	4			206	12800	721	4728	22.95	10	3	62.14
44 80	Adelaide	26.0	4	74	-			206	12956	725	4802	23.31	10	3	62.89
81		25.4	11	60	1	GP Wickramasinghe	bowled	207	13110	736	4862	23.48	10	3	63.33
		27.0	11	68	1			207	13118	736	4870	23.53	10	3	63.37
1996-97 v West Indies in Australia															
45 82	Brisbane	26.0	3	80	1	IR Bishop	lbw	208	13274	739	4950	23.79	10	3	63.81
		27.0	3	88	2	KCG Benjamin	lbw	209	13280	739	4958	23.72	10	3	63.54
83		4.0	1	19	1	RG Samuels	ct MA Taylor	210	13304	740	4977	23.70	10	3	63.35
		30.2	11	67	2	JC Adams	lbw	211	13462	750	5025	23.81	10	3	63.80
		41.0	16	92	2			211	13526	755	5050	23.93	10	3	64.10
46 84	Sydney	20.3	9	28	1	CL Hooper	lbw	212	13649	764	5078	23.95	10	3	64.38
		26.3	12	40	2	S Chanderpaul	ct SK Warne	213	13685	767	5090	23.89	10	3	64.24
		35.2	13	65	3	IR Bishop	ct MTG Elliott	214	13738	768	5115	23.90	10	3	64.20
85		3.4	2	5	1	RG Samuels	bowled	215	13760	770	5120	23.81	10	3	64.00
		13.5	2	65	2	S Chanderpaul	bowled	216	13821	770	5180	23.98	10	3	63.98
		25.0	5	77	3	KCG Benjamin	ct MA Taylor	217	13888	773	5192	23.92	10	3	64.00
		27.4	5	95	4	CA Walsh	ct GD McGrath	218	13904	773	5210	23.90	10	3	63.78
47 86	Melbourne	5.3	2	7	1	RG Samuels	ct MA Taylor	219	13937	775	5217	23.82	10	3	63.63
		22.2	3	50	2	CEL Ambrose	bowled	220	14038	776	5260	23.90	10	3	63.80
		28.1	3	72	3	CA Walsh	ct ME Waugh	221	14073	776	5282	23.90	10	3	63.68
87		3.0	-	17	-			221	14091	776	5299	23.98	10	3	63.76
48 88	Adelaide	0.4	-	1	1	BC Lara	ct GS Blewett	222	14095	776	5300	23.87	10	3	63.49
		2.0	-	7	2	S Chanderpaul	ct MA Taylor	223	14107	776	5206	23.34	10	3	63.26
		12.0	3	30	3	JC Adams	bowled	224	14163	779	5329	23.79	10	3	63.22
		16.0	4	42	3			224	14187	780	5341	23.84	10	3	63.33
89		10.0	1	40	1	CL Hooper	lbw	225	14247	781	5381	23.91	10	3	63.32
		12.3	2	46	2	IR Bishop	ct MG Bevan	226	14262	782	5387	23.83	10	3	63.10

Tst	Inn	Venue	Ovrs	Md	Rns	Wk	Batsman	How Out	Wkt	Balls	Mds	Runs	Avrge	5	10	Stk/Rt
1996-97 v West Indies in Australia (cont.)																
48	89	Adel'de (cont.)	16.3	4	52	3	BC Lara	ct IA Healy	227	14286	784	5393	23.75	10	3	62.93
			20.0	4	68	3			227	14307	784	5409	23.83	10	3	63.03
49	90	Perth	11.3	4	43	1	BC Lara	ct IA Healy	228	14376	788	5452	23.91	10	3	63.05
			15.3	6	48	2	RG Samuels	ct ME Waugh	229	14400	790	5457	23.82	10	3	62.88
			19.0	8	55	2			229	14421	792	5464	23.86	10	3	62.97
	91		-	-	-	-			229	14421	792	5464	23.86	10	3	62.97
1996-97 v South Africa in South Africa																
50	92	Johannesburg	20.4	7	46	1	WJ Cronje	ct ME Waugh	230	14545	799	5510	23.95	10	3	63.23
			27.4	9	68	2	PR Adams	lbw	231	14587	801	5532	23.95	10	3	63.15
	93		3.4	2	2	1	G Kirsten	bowled	232	14609	803	5534	23.85	10	3	62.96
			7.4	4	7	2	DJ Cullinan	ct IA Healy	233	14633	805	5539	23.77	10	3	62.80
			22.3	11	35	3	JN Rhodes	lbw	234	14722	811	5567	23.79	10	3	62.91
			28.0	15	43	4	JH Kallis	bowled	235	14755	816	5575	23.72	10	3	62.79
51	94	Pt Elizabeth	18.3	5	49	1	DJ Richardson	ct GD McGrath	236	14866	821	5624	23.83	10	3	62.99
			22.4	5	61	2	BM McMillan	ct SR Waugh	237	14891	821	5636	23.78	10	3	62.83
			23.4	5	62	3	AA Donald	ct SK Warne	238	14897	821	5637	23.68	10	3	62.59
	95		13.4	5	18	1	SM Pollock	lbw	239	14979	826	5655	23.66	10	3	62.67
			17.4	7	20	2	PR Adams	ct MA Taylor	240	15003	828	5657	23.57	10	3	62.51
52	96	Centurion	36.0	11	89	-			240	15219	839	5746	23.94	10	3	63.41
	97		-	-	-	-			240	15219	839	5746	23.94	10	3	63.41

BATTING

Opponents	Debut	M	Inn	NO	Runs	H.S	0s	50	100	Avrge	Ct
India	1991-92	2	4	1	28	20	1	-	-	9.33	1
Sri Lanka	1992-93	5	4	-	99	35	-	-	-	24.75	6
New Zealand	1992-93	6	6	3	134	74*	-	1	-	44.67	5
England	1993	11	15	3	173	37	3	-	-	14.42	9
South Africa	1993-94	9	14	1	99	18	2	-	-	7.62	5
Pakistan	1994-95	6	8	1	108	33	1	-	-	15.43	2
West Indies	1994-95	13	19	-	198	30	4	-	-	10.42	11
Total		52	70	9	839	74*	11	1	-	13.75	39

HIGHEST SCORE

74* Australia v New Zealand, Brisbane, 1993-94

INTERNATIONAL LIMITED-OVERS

Debut: 1992-93 Australia v New Zealand, Wellington

BOWLING

Season	M	Balls	Mdns	Runs	Wkts	Avrge	5	Best	Stk/Rt
1992-93	1	60	-	40	2	20.00	-	2/40	30.00
1993-94	21	1128	9	689	42	16.40	-	4/19	26.86
1994-95	21	1227	16	824	28	29.43	-	4/40	43.82
1995-96	16	892	10	580	27	21.48	-	4/34	33.04
1996-97	14	779	8	597	29	20.59	1	5/33	26.86
Total	73	4086	43	2730	128	21.33	1	5/33	31.92

RECORD AGAINST EACH COUNTRY

Opponents	Debut	M	Balls	Mdns	Runs	Wkts	Avrge	5	Best	Stk/Rt
New Zealand	1992-93	9	540	7	286	24	11.92	-	4/19	22.50
South Africa	1992-93	24	1275	9	907	37	24.51	-	4/36	34.46
Sri Lanka	1993-94	9	498	4	338	15	22.53	-	3/20	33.20
India	1993-94	4	234	1	182	5	36.40	-	2/40	46.80
Pakistan	1994-95	8	457	9	298	14	21.29	-	4/37	32.64
Zimbabwe	1994-95	3	171	2	84	7	12.00	-	4/34	24.43
England	1994-95	2	120	-	83	3	27.67	-	2/37	40.00
West Indies	1994-95	13	731	11	527	22	23.95	1	5/33	33.23
Kenya	1995-96	1	60	-	25	1	25.00	-	1/25	60.00

INNINGS BY INNINGS COMPARISON

	Balls	Mdns	Runs	Wkts	Avrge	5	Best	Stk/Rt
First Innings	2273	21	1486	68	21.85	-	4/19	33.43
Second Innings	1813	22	1244	60	20.73	1	5/33	30.22

RECORD IN EACH COUNTRY

Country	Debut	M	Balls	Mdns	Runs	Wkts	Avrge	5	Best	Stk/Rt
New Zealand	1992-93	5	300	6	180	7	25.71	-	2/18	42.86
Australia	1993-94	31	1709	19	1076	62	17.35	1	5/33	27.56
South Africa	1993-94	14	739	5	557	21	26.52	-	4/36	35.19
Sharjah	1993-94	3	174	1	103	9	11.44	-	4/34	19.33
Sri Lanka	1994-95	3	168	1	109	7	15.57	-	3/29	24.00
Pakistan	1994-95	7	410	4	296	6	49.33	-	4/40	68.33
West Indies	1994-95	4	235	4	204	4	51.00	-	2/33	58.75
India	1995-96	6	351	3	205	12	17.08	-	4/34	29.25

VENUES

	Debut	M	Balls	Mdns	Runs	Wkts	Avrge	5	Best	Stk/Rt
In New Zealand										
Wellington	1992-93	2	120	3	58	4	14.50	-	2/18	30.00
Auckland	1994-95	2	120	3	61	3	20.33	-	2/21	40.00
Dunedin	1994-95	1	60	-	61	-	-	-	-	-
In Australia										
Melbourne	1993-94	11	655	8	390	21	18.57	-	4/19	31.19
Adelaide	1993-94	3	161	3	99	8	12.38	-	4/25	20.13
Sydney	1993-94	10	501	6	324	23	14.09	1	5/33	21.78
Perth	1993-94	4	240	2	154	7	22.00	-	2/27	34.29
Hobart	1994-95	2	98	-	58	3	19.33	-	2/35	32.67
Brisbane	1994-95	1	54	-	51	-	-	-	-	-
In South Africa										
Johannesburg	1993-94	2	120	-	101	1	101.00	-	1/45	120.00
Verwoerdburg	1993-94	1	48	1	41	1	41.00	-	1/41	48.00
Port Elizabeth	1993-94	3	114	-	93	5	18.60	-	4/36	22.80
Durban	1993-94	2	97	3	68	3	22.67	-	2/36	32.33
East London	1993-94	2	120	-	70	3	23.33	-	2/36	40.00
Cape Town	1993-94	2	120	-	95	5	19.00	-	3/31	24.00
Bloemfontein	1993-94	1	60	-	37	1	37.00	-	1/37	60.00
Centurion	1996-97	1	60	1	52	2	26.00	-	2/52	30.00
In United Arab Emirates										
Sharjah	1993-94	3	174	1	103	9	11.44	-	4/34	19.33
In Sri Lanka										
Colombo (SSC)	1994-95	1	60	1	29	3	9.67	-	3/29	20.00
Colombo (PIS)	1994-95	1	60	-	53	2	26.50	-	2/53	30.00
Colombo (PSS)	1994-95	1	48	-	27	2	13.50	-	2/27	24.00
In Pakistan										
Lahore	1994-95	3	180	2	129	-	-	-	-	-
Multan	1994-95	1	60	1	29	1	29.00	-	1/29	60.00
Faisalabad	1994-95	1	56	-	40	4	10.00	-	4/40	14.00
Rawalpindi	1994-95	1	54	1	47	-	-	-	-	-
Peshawar	1994-95	1	60	-	51	1	51.00	-	1/51	60.00
In West Indies										
Bridgetown	1994-95	1	60	-	56	1	56.00	-	1/56	60.00
Port-of-Spain	1994-95	2	120	1	115	1	115.00	-	1/63	120.00
Kingston	1994-95	1	55	3	33	2	16.50	-	2/33	27.50
In India										
Visakhapatnam	1995-96	1	60	-	25	1	25.00	-	1/25	60.00
Mumbai	1995-96	1	60	1	28	1	28.00	-	1/28	60.00
Nagpur	1995-96	1	57	1	34	4	8.50	-	4/34	14.25
Jaipur	1995-96	1	60	1	30	-	-	-	-	-
Chennai	1995-96	1	60	-	52	2	26.00	-	2/52	30.00
Chandigarh	1995-96	1	54	-	36	4	9.00	-	4/36	13.50

BATTING

Opponents	Debut	M	Inn	NO	Runs	H.S	0s	50	100	Avrge	Stk/Rt	Ct
New Zealand	1992-93	9	3	-	36	24	-	-	-	12.00	116.13	5
South Africa	1992-93	24	16	4	168	55	2	1	-	14.00	80.38	8
Sri Lanka	1993-94	9	2	1	5	3*	-	-	-	5.00	55.56	1
India	1993-94	4	4	1	10	5*	1	-	-	3.33	38.46	-
Pakistan	1994-95	8	6	1	69	30	-	-	-	13.80	71.88	3
Zimbabwe	1994-95	3	1	-	5	5	-	-	-	5.00	100.00	1
England	1994-95	2	1	-	21	21	-	-	-	21.00	84.00	1
West Indies	1994-95	13	6	4	41	12	-	-	-	20.50	105.13	5
Kenya	1995-96	1	1	1	0	0*	-	-	-	-	0.00	-
Total		73	40	12	355	55	3	1	-	12.68	80.32	24

HIGHEST SCORE

55 (58) Australia v South Africa, Port Elizabeth, 1993-94

MARK RAY

When The Bushrangers play the **NSW** Blues it's traditionally a grudge match – but the young **NSW** fans don't let that get in the way of the spirit of the game.

SHEFFIELD SHIELD

Debut: 1990-91 Victoria v Western Australia, St Kilda

BOWLING

Season	M	Balls	Mdns	Runs	Wkts	Avrge	5	10	Best	Stk/Rt
1990-91	1	222	13	102	1	102.00	-	-	1/41	222.00
1991-92	6	1341	65	569	12	47.42	-	-	4/75	111.75
1992-93	4	909	24	486	12	40.50	1	-	5/49	75.75
1993-94	4	1486	64	643	27	23.81	2	-	6/42	55.03
1994-95	2	703	39	265	13	20.38	1	-	5/104	54.07
1995-96	3	1021	36	426	11	38.73	1	-	5/122	92.81
1996-97	2	582	31	201	5	40.20	-	-	3/25	116.40
Total	22	6264	272	2692	81	33.23	5	-	6/42	77.33

Opponents	Debut	M	Balls	Mdns	Runs	Wkts	Avrge	5	10	Best	Stk/Rt
Western Australia	1990-91	5	1441	70	584	23	25.39	2	-	6/42	62.65
Tasmania	1991-92	3	817	43	296	14	21.14	1	-	5/104	58.35
New South Wales	1991-92	7	1903	74	947	25	37.88	2	-	5/77	76.12
South Australia	1991-92	4	1167	55	466	11	42.36	-	-	4/119	106.09
Queensland	1992-93	3	936	30	399	8	49.88	-	-	3/111	117.00

BEST BOWLING

Wkts	Opponent	Venue	Series
5/49	Western Australia	St Kilda	1992-93
6/42	Western Australia	Melbourne	1993-94
5/77	New South Wales	Sydney	1993-94
5/104	Tasmania	Melbourne	1994-95
5/122	New South Wales	Melbourne	1995-96

BATTING

Opponents	Debut	M	Inn	NO	Runs	H.S	0s	50	100	Avrge	Ct
Western Australia	1990-91	5	6	-	96	69	1	1	-	16.00	2
Tasmania	1991-92	3	4	1	56	34	-	-	-	18.67	1
New South Wales	1991-92	7	10	-	174	52	1	1	-	17.40	5
South Australia	1991-92	4	5	1	64	30*	1	-	-	16.00	1
Queensland	1992-93	3	4	2	27	15*	1	-	-	13.50	4
Total		22	29	4	417	69	4	2	-	16.68	13

HIGHEST SCORE

69 Victoria v Western Australia, St Kilda, 1992-93

DOMESTIC LIMITED-OVERS

Debut: 1992-93 Victoria v Tasmania, Devonport

BOWLING

Opponents	Debut	M	Balls	Mdns	Runs	Wkts	Avrge	5	Best	Stk/Rt
Tasmania	1992-93	2	95	1	66	8	8.25	1	5/35	11.88
Queensland	1993-94	2	114	1	96	1	96.00	-	1/36	114.00
South Australia	1993-94	3	180	3	113	4	28.25	-	2/34	45.00
New South Wales	1995-96	1	18	-	17	-	-	-	-	-
Western Australia	1995-96	2	120	2	68	2	34.00	-	2/17	60.00
Total		10	527	7	360	15	24.00	1	5/35	35.13

BEST BOWLING

5/35 Victoria v Tasmania, Carlton, 1996-97

BATTING

Opponents	Debut	M	Inn	NO	Runs	H.S	0s	50	100	Avrge	Stk/Rt	Ct
Tasmania	1992-93	2	1	-	26	26	-	-	-	26.00	76.47	3
Queensland	1993-94	2	-	-	-	-	-	-	-	-	-	1
South Australia	1993-94	3	2	1	44	32	-	-	-	44.00	115.79	3
New South Wales	1995-96	1	1	-	5	5	-	-	-	5.00	71.43	-
Western Australia	1995-96	2	2	-	15	15	1	-	-	7.50	51.72	-
Total		10	6	1	90	32	1	-	-	18.00	83.33	7

HIGHEST SCORE

32 (26) Victoria v South Australia, Adelaide, 1994-95

STEVE CHRISTO/THE FAIRFAX PHOTO LIBRARY